Tales of
TIME & TIDE

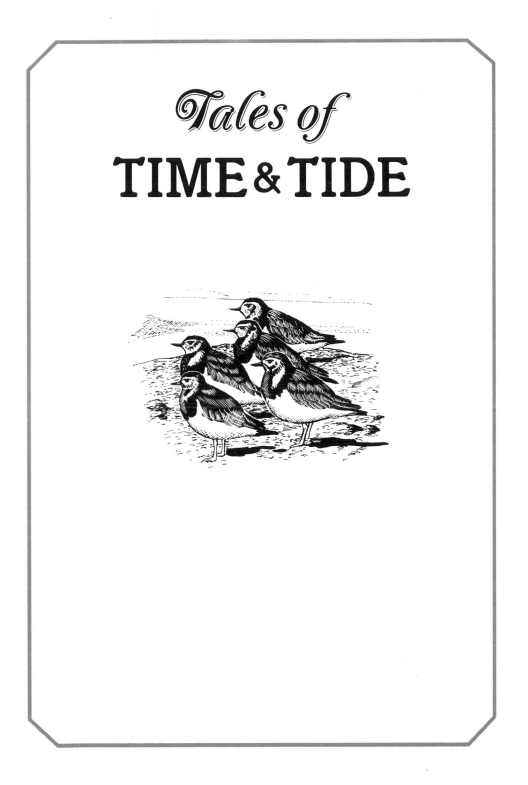

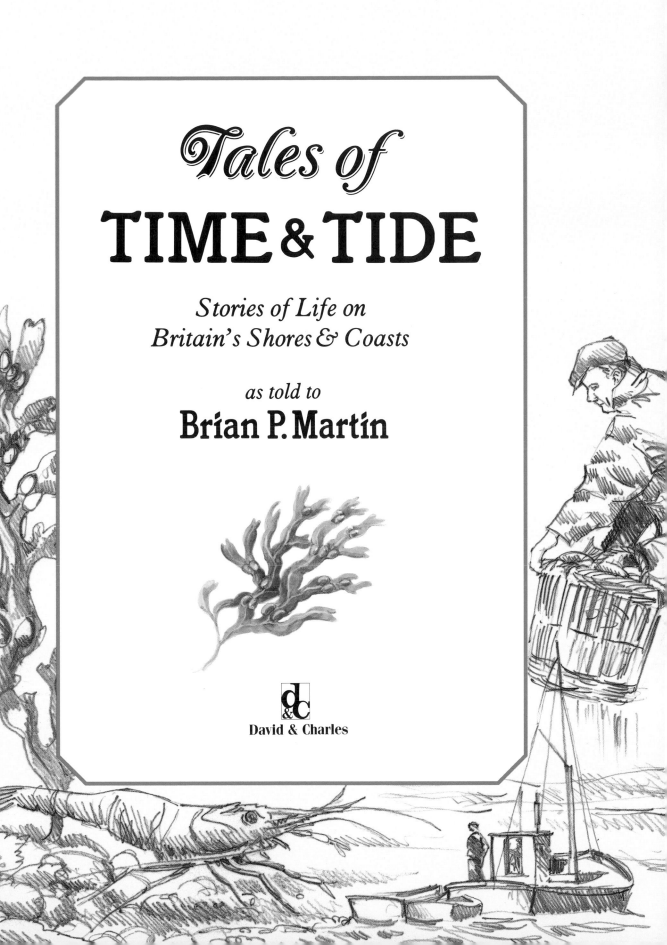

Tales of
TIME & TIDE

Stories of Life on
Britain's Shores & Coasts

as told to
Brian P. Martin

David & Charles

ALSO BY BRIAN MARTIN

Tales of the Old Countrymen
Tales of the Old Gamekeepers
More Tales of the Old Gamekeepers
Wildfowl of the British Isles and North-West Europe
Birds of Prey of the British Isles
Sporting Birds of Britain and Ireland
The Glorious Grouse
World Birds
The Great Shoots
British Gameshooting, Roughshooting and Wildfowling
The Art of Game Cookery (with Rosemary Wadey)

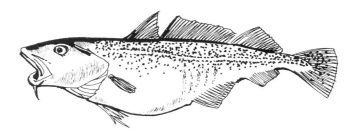

Illustrations by Philip Murphy

A DAVID & CHARLES BOOK
Copyright © text Brian P. Martin 1994
First published 1994

A catalogue record for this book is available from the
British Library.

ISBN 0 7153 0050 4

Typeset by Ace Filmsetting Ltd, Frome, Somerset
and printed in Great Britain
by Butler & Tanner Ltd, Frome for David & Charles
Brunel House   Newton Abbot   Devon

CONTENTS

BETWEEN THE TIDES

There is a land where no man lives,
  yet all the world is there;
a kingdom which creation gives
  to wash away all care.

It is the seat of ancient dreams,
  a realm of dancing light,
alive in sunshine and moonbeams,
  a stage to set us right.

This place is the haunt of wild things,
  where all souls can abide,
and horizons gleam with hope in
  the tales of time and tide.

BRIAN MARTIN, 1993

INTRODUCTION

BRITAIN'S coast is one of the most interesting in the world. It may not have what many people regard as idyllic beaches, truly dynamic scenery or the richness of wildlife found in other, more remote climes, but its variety and history are second to none. Shakespeare's 'sceptred isle' is *the* home of seafarers, and no other nation is more conscious of the increasing importance of its coast.

In the beginning Man simply sought to harvest the sea as he did the land, so our coast was primarily a workplace. Then when our ancestors started to peer over the horizon, the sea became a highway and our coast spawned safe havens from which the world could be explored and conquered. However, other nations had similar ideas, so our coast also had to serve as a main line of defence. And as Britain's fishing and trading fleets grew, so too did the navy required to protect them; thus many of our ports became fortresses. But in the nineteenth and twentieth centuries our inshore waters and coasts have become equally important for two other reasons – recreation and conservation. As inland Britain has become congested, Man has increasingly looked to the sea for a new playground and a glimpse of rapidly disappearing wilderness.

But whether founded on subsistence or sport, all these interests have attracted employment, not least the shoals of jobs created by the network of safety and emergency services now necessary to safeguard all. This book reflects the surprisingly wide variety of these coastal occupations.

Through tracing the lives of sixteen great characters, using their own colourful language wherever possible, I have sought to provide an insight into Britain's coastal heritage. My subjects, aged fifty-seven to eighty-eight, have spent most of their lives by the sea and some are still working in their seventies. Even those who have hung up their seaboots for the last time remain firmly attached to the briny. Lighthouse keeper John Burrage reflected their feelings: 'I could never live away from the sea. I like to be able to open a door or window and see it any time I want.'

Sadly, the days of manned lighthouses are numbered. With economy at the helm, automation is the order of the day. Understandably, many young skippers with sophisticated new navigational equipment no longer wish to pay for what they regard as clinging to the past. Yet their fathers drew great comfort from that simple flash of light on the black headland, and knew that the men behind it were much more than automatons: they were kingpins of coastal society.

Others, too, are on the way out. Brendan Sellick and Tony Brewer will almost certainly be the last two fishermen to ride their strange 'mud-horses' across Bridgwater Bay. And it is already decades since Hebridean postmen such as Archie Macdonald delivered Britain's mail by horseback across tidal waters, or tough Yorkshiremen such as Ned Chandler hung over the clifftop to harvest birds' eggs.

Yet some ancient ways continue to have a bright future. Indeed, the Fal oyster fishery still thrives because the local council does not allow shellfishermen to use craft with engines. As a result, western Europe's sole surviving fleet of working sailboats still graces Cornish waters, and men such as Frank Vinnicombe continue to enjoy the tradition of their grandfathers.

Others have been forced to adapt. For example, Dorset swanherd and decoyman Dick Dalley once reared swans for the table, as monks did centuries before him, but now he cares for the birds in order to nourish Man's spirit rather than his body. And stalwarts such as National Trust warden Leslie Hicks have used their great practical experience of coast and countryside to benefit the new conservation movement.

Fishing continues to be a mainstay of the coastal community, but now that fish stocks are dwindling and British waters are besieged by European vessels there is growing chaos and concern. Even as I write, controversy rages over Government plans to restrict British boats to fishing on certain days. Undoubtedly many more storms are already brewing over the horizon, but there is no denying that urgent steps must be taken to conserve fish populations.

Coastal wildlife and habitat are threatened too, not only by ghastly oil and chemical pollution, but also by the very people who love our heritage. All of us who catch fish, shoot wildfowl, sail boards and boats, watch birds or simply sunbathe or ramble, increase disturbance of numerous species. And because there are so many of us even the footpaths are wearing away in places.

With so many pressures on our coast it is essential that we continue to support organisations such as the National Trust, whose Enterprise Neptune is doing so much to protect our heritage. But it's not simply a question of dropping coins into the collection box to purchase a few more precious acres. Coast as well as countryside must be managed properly, to the benefit of Man as well as wildlife. And in this there is much to learn from the sages who form the backbone of my book. Leslie Hicks needs no telling that re-establishment of grazing headlands will grow good meat as well as orchids, and fishermen such as Fred Marr have never doubted the need to clamp down on trawling and regularly 'rest' every section of seabed so that there is something for next season.

Our coast must be protected at all costs, to Man's spiritual as well as material advantage. Having grown up on the coast I can never resist the opportunity to catch a fish, but more importantly I value the chance to walk along the clifftop or sit by the shore thinking about nothing in particular. And when I'm too old even to shuffle along the shingle, no doubt I'll join the ranks of those lined up in their cars, staring out to sea and wondering about what once was. For all the years I have lived inland the sound of the surf has never left my ears. Like any other Briton, I have more salt than blood in my body; but few of us have such great love and understanding of the coast as that displayed by the sixteen characters now put before you.

BRIAN MARTIN
BROOK, SURREY
1993

END OF THE LINE

NED CHANDLER

*LAST OF YORKSHIRE'S CLIFF-CLIMBING
EGG HARVESTERS*

Herring gull egg

Guillemot egg

FOR those of us who turn green merely on approaching the edge of an unfenced cliff, the prospect of dangling over the sheer rock face is enough to inspire nightmares. Yet as late as the 1950s there were a handful of Yorkshiremen who happily did this for a living. These hardy 'climmers' had a well-established market for the thousands of seabird eggs regularly laid on local cliff ledges, and such rich pickings could not be ignored by families desperate to supplement meagre incomes during difficult times. Indeed, it took strengthening of the law rather than development of fear to end this centuries-old natural harvesting. With the introduction of tougher bird-protection legislation in 1954 this way of life ceased for ever. For Ned Chandler it was a particularly precipitous end to a proud family tradition for, like his father and grandfather before him, he had spent most of his working life cheating death on Bempton's 400-foot cliffs. Now Ned is again at the end of the line, but in a different way: he is the last man alive who regularly clawed a living from England's cliffs.

'I was fourteen when I first went over the edge. I wasn't scared—I 'adn't to be! Dad simply said: "Come on, you're next". But it was perfectly safe as long as you stuck to the rules, had some good hobnails in your boots and kept your equipment in order. Also, it was best to stick to one main climmer in the gang of four so that he got really used to it and knew every ledge.

'The only local man who ever died from it was Joss Major of Flamborough. Even he would have lived if he'd worn proper head protection, as most people did. In the days before Army-surplus tin hats, which came in after the Great War, each climmer wore a hard hat stuffed with grass or straw, but Major insisted on

The 'old gang' of climmers (1 to r): David Cross, William Hodgson, George Hodgson and Henry Chandler

wearing a flat cap. So when a small stone fell on him from a considerable height he was killed.

'I never had any falls or injuries, but once Dad was off a fortnight when a boulder badly bruised his ribs. Another time his thumb was knocked out of place, but his head was OK as he always wore a policeman's cork helmet. Harold Robson, who was the main climmer in my gang—the last—always wore a tin hat. When I was younger there were three gangs at Bempton plus three main climming families at Flamborough. Now I'm the only man left.'

Christened John Edward, Ned was born at Bempton on 23 January 1914, the eldest of six children, all of whom were still alive in 1993. His father and grandfather were farm labourers, who took unpaid leave for the short climming season in May and June. But the seasonal work was well worthwhile because a climmer could easily earn six times as much as a farm worker.

Thus it was not surprising that Ned was milking cows from the age of seven. 'I used to fetch 'em up after school, then stop on to milk 'em, for about a shilling a week. It was a very hard life then, with father in and out of work all the time. His wages were only twenty-five shillings a week, but we had our own house, which was Grandad's. With it was an acre of land and we used to feed a few pigs up to sell. I helped Dad with the killing: he'd stun an animal, then blade it. After that we'd scald it to get the hairs off, hang it up on a rope to dry, then cut it up next day and sell it round the houses. Mother cured hams with saltpetre and hung them from the beams in the livin' room.'

Ned's earliest memories of the sea concern two wrecks, for the same craggy coastline which attracts the birds has long been a graveyard for ships. The first incident happened in 1926, when Ned was eleven. 'The big Italian ship *Radium* got too near the coast when trying to avoid the worst of a storm and foundered under the cliffs. We pulled the rocket cart up to the clifftop and looked straight down the ship's two funnels, she was so close in.

'We managed to get a line over her from the top and all the crew were saved. The skipper gave us some biscuits as big as dinner plates, but they were so 'ard you 'ad to steep 'em in water. All the coal was thrown overboard but the tugs still couldn't move *Radium*, so it was decided to blow her up with dynamite a few weeks later. Her boilers are still there.'

The other wreck was in 1931. 'The trawler *Skegness* was at anchor, sheltering from a storm, with thunder and lightning. They radioed for assistance from Filey lifeboat, but were told they were all right. Unfortunately the wind suddenly changed right round, blew them in towards the cliff and a big wave broke the wheelhouse, killing 'em all.

'The horse-drawn rocket cart came out the three miles or so from Speeton and tried to fire a line from the clifftop over the wreck below. But the wind blew it back, so Father climbed down the cliff and got a line out from below. But it was too late. Eleven men drowned and we helped bring their bodies ashore over the next few weeks. One man we found just had his hands sticking out the gravel along the beach—weeks later. All the bodies had to be put in bags, pulled up the cliff and carried by stretcher to an ambulance waiting in a field nearby. There was no other access because the sea never goes out from that part of the cliffs.

'Another thing us climmers used to help out with was suicides. The police used to come and we 'ad to fetch the bodies up from the places where the tide never leaves.'

On leaving Bempton school at fourteen, Ned lived and worked full-time on a farm about three miles away. 'I worked a minimum of from 7am to 5pm for £9 a year and did absolutely everythin', from dippin' sheep and milkin' cows to cuttin' the corn with a binder and workin' lovely Shire horses.

'After that I worked on about three local farms, right up to 1949, when I married Joyce. I didn't have to join up because farming was a reserved occupation, but I saw some action all right. Aye, this was a fighter area this was. German bombers used to get their bearings with the flash of Flamborough

Ned's father, Henry, wore a policeman's helmet to protect against falling rocks dislodged by his rope. He is seen here with some of the prized guillemot eggs

lighthouse. A lot were shot down by Spitfires—I saw several get it. And a land mine destroyed the post office at Brigg: several postal workers were killed.

'Then I went on the railway and doubled me money. In 1965 I went into engineering and doubled me pay again. I retired in 1979 at the age of sixty-five, but I had to stop climming when the law changed in 1954.

'Nobody local wanted us to stop climming and all the visitors wanted us to keep up. People would often walk out for a mile or more just to watch. We were out on Sundays too, and at Whitsuntide there'd be a big enough crowd for a whip-round with the cap. Ooh aye! Ooh aye!'

Sometimes visitors asked if they could have a go at the climming, and even paid for the 'privilege'. It is said that the more unscrupulous gangs took the money first, knowing that some people would back out at the last moment. But even those folk brave enough to have a go usually made a mess of it.

Ned particularly remembers two mountain climbers who came along and said: 'That looks easy'. 'We didn't like 'em at all so we put 'em over Jubilee, where you can still see the stakes Grandad drove in to get round the overhang. When they came back up all their knees were ripped open and they scurried off without sayin' anything. They didn't pay.

'Back in the 1940s Reg Dixon the TV man came to record the sound of the birds nestin'. So we put 'im down the cliff to a green patch of grass, fastened the rope to a stake and went away to watch from the side. But as we went round he counted us and when he realised no one was left at the top he soon yelled out. We 'ad to go back immediately. He said: "By gum, I were a pilot durin' the war but this is the most scared I've ever been".

'Our main ropes were 300ft long and we had two big pulleys set in the cliff edge. The climmer also had a leather harness and a guide rope. The bloke who controlled the rope at the top had a leather belt and he could feel every jerk—one for more hand rope and three to come up.

'The hemp ropes were made locally at Kilham, cost about £5 each and lasted two seasons, after which we sold 'em to farmers to keep sheaves of corn on the wagons. The ropes were heavy so at the end of each day we'd put them in a bag and bury them in a hole with a grass sod over in a sheltered bank on the cliff. We only took them home at the end of the season.

'About fifteen minutes was spent gathering the eggs on each pitch or "down", but there was no rest before moving on to the next. The climmer had to have strong legs and use his feet all the time: he soon got skinned if he didn't.'

The egg harvest changed little during Ned's time, the men being very careful to 'rest a patch of cliff each year, to ensure that the birds came back'. There has been a substantial increase in some local seabird populations since climming stopped, but this is at least partly due to other factors such as natural range expansion.

'The climmer carried two bags: one for the big tough eggs, another for the more fragile, smaller ones. The main eggs taken were scout (guillemot), razorbill, kittiwake, puffin, fulmar and herring gull. Kittiwake eggs fetched about tuppence each and mostly went to the baker's because they were very rich and good for custards. But best were the guillemots', which fetched sixpence each when hens'

Guillemots: providers of the most desirable eggs

eggs were only a penny. Just one would fill a frying pan. Aye, when you'd had a guillemot's egg you were full. People used to come to the house for guillemot eggs. They were very good food and we sold as many as we could get. They were specially welcome during the war.

'A guillemot only lays one egg, but will replace it twice if it is taken. We'd go round a patch every three days: then we knew the eggs were fresh. An egg would last for a year stood on its point—so that you get the yolk in the middle—in an egg tray in the pantry. I've kept quite a few to Christmas and they've been good.

'A guillemot sits with her egg on her feet, and not many eggs get broken through falling off because they are pear-shaped and roll round in tiny circles. You had

Counting the haul from Bempton cliffs are the 'young gang'. Ned is nearest, with his back to the camera

to be careful not to frighten the birds else a few eggs would get pushed over the edge, but they didn't sit tight on our gatherin' patches.

'It were only a short season, but we'd earn £10 a week each, and all we had to give the farmer whose land we were on was about two dozen guillemots' eggs each year. During the best times we had twenty-odd dozen eggs a day and there was always people waitin' for 'em when we got home at tea-time. But if it had been raining we often had to go out after tea to make up, as you couldn't work safely when it was wet. We only ever worked in good weather and didn't go out in storms or severe cold. The worst winter and early spring I can remember in these parts was in 1947 when you could only just creep under Dotterem railway bridge, the snow was so deep. Usually there was 15ft headway there. The buses didn't run for weeks.'

Collectors, too, were interested in the eggs. Some were local children who hung about the clifftop hoping to get the more common varieties for little or nothing, but others were very serious and had plenty of money to spend. They came from as far as Birmingham, but the one Ned remembers most was '. . . Mr Henshaw, the surveyor from Wellingborough, who had a lovely collection. I think the most he paid for an egg was £2 in 1940, for a beautiful turquoise blue guillemot egg without a mark on it.

'Another guillemot egg we had was an extra-long blue one with unusual markings. The same bird laid one just the same every year for thirteen years and Mr Henshaw bought the lot. But Mr Lupton the barrister was just as keen: he used to come and stop for a whole month in the village. They all come bed and breakfast in the thirties and forties.

'The collectors wanted all types of egg, not just the ones you eat. For example, we had quite a few kestrels on the cliffs and a whole clutch of theirs fetched about £1.

'Puffins could be a bit of a problem because they'd peck your fingers when you shoved your 'and in their burrow. Many's the time me Dad pulled 'is 'and out with a puffin on the end of it. So 'e made a long-handled spoon thing to get round it.

'Fulmars would dive and spit at you. They'd cough three times and the third time you 'ad to watch out because then they'd shoot a foul, oily substance which smelled of petrol. A good defence.

'The first gannet seen in the area came in May 1923, when I was nine. The following year he or she got a mate and nested. I was at the cliff the day Willie Hodgson spotted it. Mr Henshaw, who identified it, was so pleased he gave Willie £1. "Here you are Willie", he said. "Buy yourself a drink".' This was fourteen years before the first official record of gannets nesting at Bempton.

Today Ned and Joyce, who have no children, live quietly in retirement at the village of Sewerby, just three miles from those challenging heights. The wild cries of seabirds and crashing of surf may still ring in Ned's ears, but now Yorkshire's own Tarzan clings only to memories rather than rock. All the climmers have gone to roost and their ancient haunt has become an RSPB bird reserve.

FROM THE ARCHIVES

Dangerous Feat

ANOTHER constant source of danger is the detaching of small pieces of rock or loose stones, by the friction of the rope against the cliff: to avoid these, the cliff-man has to keep an incessant lookout, and to bob his head this way and that, to escape a broken sconce.

From *The Letters of Rusticus* (1849)

Flaming Head

THE little point whose bend forms this bay is called vulgarly Flamborough Head, by writers who say that Ida the Saxon, who first reduced this country, landed here. Some think it took its name from a lighthouse, which in the night pointed out the port by flame. For the Britans still retain the word flam from their provincial language, and sailors mark this place in their charts with a flaming head.

From William Camden's *Britannia* (1586, revised 1789)

RICH WITH A HA'PENNY

MURDO MACLEOD

CROFTER AND FISHERMAN OF THE ISLE OF SKYE

Seaweed was the best top dressing for grass to grow

WHILE two world wars raged and the twentieth century spawned dollar worship, Murdo Macleod clung to one of the Western world's few remaining outposts of true civilisation. And while more restless men sailed the seven seas in search of gold, or at least shunted about the kingdom trying to turn sixpence into a sovereign, this real heir to The Isles remained disarmingly content. He admits that for some years he had nothing in his pocket but holes, and if he had a ha'penny he was rich; but on magical Skye his wealth has always been greater than money.

Now in his eighties, Murdo has never been to England. The furthest he has been is Edinburgh '. . . a lovely city. I liked to go in June when the work was slack and the flowers beautiful. And many's the time I went there when the corn was in and the stacks secured.

'I did go to Inverness once, when I had to attend the tribunal to see if I had to go to war. Before I went I was getting sheets and sheets of paper asking me about my life, but in the end they decided I didn't have to fight because my work on the land was more important to support the soldiers. It was safe enough up here, but we still had the blackout in the war. Nothing came, but when Glasgow was bombed we thought we could see a glare in the sky.

'I made that journey to Inverness on the train and remember it well because when I left it was blowin' a gale of wind—but on the other side I had to pull the blinds down, it was so bright. The weather is very different between east and west.'

Twelve-year-old Murdo and his sister Maryann, at Struan Public school, in 1926

Perhaps Murdo would have ventured further afield if he had managed to get a driving licence. 'I went for the test eight times, but was very unlucky, especially the first time in Portree, which was so busy because they were holding the Games there.'

But even if Murdo had been able to drive as a young man he would have found Skye's rudimentary routes somewhat testing. 'When I was a boy anyone going away to Portree had to go in carriages with big wheels strong enough to manage the rough roads. Floods often took away the gravel and left big stones sticking out. Horses were the best local transport, though later on I did have a 650cc Triumph motorbike, which was the only sure cure for the midges!'

One of eight children and christened Murdoch, Murdo was born on 14 April 1914 at Struanmore, within a short walk of his present home at Ullinish, overlooking Loch Bracadale, on Skye's west coast. His father and grandfather worked on local farms before these were split into crofts.

'With all the work on the land there were a lot more houses and people in these parts then, so we managed to get about forty children at Struan Public School. I'd sooner have been away to the fields, but there was the compulsory officer and if you were away from school more than a few days he would reach the house and warn the parents. Lessons were murder for me, especially as I couldn't speak a word of English when I started. It was always the Gaelic at home. Even now I sometimes have to think carefully about the right word.

'We were all very poor then. The only lighting was paraffin lamps and candles, and it was always peat for the fire. As a young boy I had no idea how much work was attached to the peat cutting, but later I had to help for a few hours after school. It was awful, with all the midges biting, and some of the upper peats were very hard to cut.

'Peat cutting always took place when the main land work was done, maybe at the end of April or beginning of May. When I stood down in the bank there was a certain way of sliding the peats up into position, and I could put eleven out without shifting.

'The peats were left there for seven to ten days and when the top was dried they were stacked in fours on end, with another in the gap and one on top. Then, if the drying was good, we could get them up to the house by horse and cart within a week. But they still had to be stacked for a long time before burning.

'There was no water in the house—it had to be carried from the well in two pails. But at least the air was good. I remember one house at Struan where you could hear the people but you couldn't see them because there was an open fire in the middle of the room and no chimney. When I went there as a boy my eyes was waterin' so much I had to run out; but those used to it were all right.

'We used to thatch our own houses then. First we used the hard rushes from three or four miles away, at Ammer, but later on I used the finer goat rush.'

The local diet consisted mostly of home-grown potatoes, loch-caught fish, and porridge. 'There was always lots of porridge and brose. We put the oatmeal and salt in a great big pot and the longer you kept it stirrin' the tastier it would be, though twenty minutes would do. You took a mouthful of porridge and dipped it in a bowl of milk. And there were always plenty of oatcakes and scones.

Lifetime crofter: Murdo outside his house in 1993. To the left are the
remains of his earlier dwelling

'We were very self-sufficient and grew our own oats as well as turnips, potatoes and other vegetables. And our souming [the number of animals allowed to be kept] was four cows and their followers [calves plus yearlings], which meant a total of twelve. But most people usually couldn't keep the yearlings on because they needed the money.

'A lot of brown seaweed was used then. We carted it up to the fields early in the year after it was washed up on the shore by the winter gales. Another sort was cut with scythes at low tide, made into rafts and pulled by boat to the nearest part suitable to get it onto the land. This had lots of bulbs on it and us children used to take them home and dry them to have fun with the caileachs, the old grandmothers. The bulbs would pop when we threw them in the fire.

'Seaweed was the best top dressing for the grass to grow. We'd spread it out with the four-pronged fork. Potatoes grew very well with it, too. And there was another type—feamain cheiran—which we could get to within one hour of the ebb tide. This was boiled with turnip, potato and oats to make a juice that the animals would drink out of pails. It was a very good medicine. If you had an old cow or horse which couldn't chew, it could live on that for a long time and still have good condition.

'Father took this croft in 1922. When Alan Macaskill's farm broke up we had twenty-four acres, but other crofts were up to about thirty acres. Ullinish had seventeen crofts then. They had a sheep stock club and bought the animals between them. Each croft has been rented from the Department of Agriculture, at first for about £10 every November and May term. I took over from Father and now I've made this croft over to my niece because I never got married—I was the wise one!'

In those days both farming and transport depended on horses, so it was as well that Murdo 'loved' them even before he went to school. 'There was one at almost every door then—mostly for workin' but also for long journeys.'

When Murdo left school at fourteen and started to work for his father it was not surprising that he did not receive any wages because 'Father had none of his own. But later on, when there was time, I also worked my two heavy Highland ponies for other people and then I was paid. When I carted manure with one horse I received 7/6d a day, from 7am to 6pm, but when two horses were needed for ploughing—there was lots of that, planting potatoes and pulling the harrows—the pay was 15s a day.'

With so many horses around there were many more blacksmiths. Murdo remembers how much he learned from Malcolm Macaskill, who lived close by, at No 10 Ullinish. 'I'd dive on a scone after school and rush down to watch him. After he went I had to go ten miles, all the way over to Dunvegan, to get new shoes for two horses—I had a saddle on one—before starting the spring ploughing. They would last through till I carried home the peats by the first week in June.

'Later there were still two or three old smiths on Skye, but not shoeing, so I started to do this when I was about thirty, while still working on the croft. People used to come and fetch me in their old cars to shoe a horse at the other end of the island. I became a registered farrier and as such had to go anywhere when called out. I even went up to help John Macleod on Lewis.

'We always had our own boat. There used to be lots of haddock out here in the middle of the loch. Once I went out with my brother at 4am for just two hours, when there was a lot of work on the land to do, and we had hundreds of fish.

'There was also lots of mackerel, saithe [coal-fish] and herring, but you can hardly get the one now. And there were plenty of small cuddies—sweet fish which you could get off the rocks with a rod.

'The haddock were caught on mussel bait with long handlines and a lead weight with a 2½ft wire through. When the weight hit the bottom you lifted it up quick for about two fathoms. You had a twist of line round your

'I also worked my two heavy Highland ponies for other people'

finger and held it clear of the boat. It was nothing to pull in two haddock at a time, and the farther you went out the bigger the fish were.

'We took mackerel with a darrow—a long gut line with nine hooks on—and often brought in nine fish at one haul. But when you had that many in the bottom of the boat all jumpin' around it was a job to get untangled. Then you lost a lot of fishing time, so in the end I cut down to three hooks.

'We made our own mackerel feathers from anything to hand. Say we had a dog with long white hair, we'd take a bunch of that. And there was always plenty of seagull and grouse feathers.

'I don't think the numbers of birds overall has changed much up here. But there used to be a lot more starlings. They made a terrible noise coming in to roost and chatterin' in the rocks by the house. You could hardly see the sky with them flying down to the ground and back again, but now they use the electricity wires.'

Murdo was 'at the lobster fishing' on Loch Bracadale with his brother about fives years after he left school. 'We made all our own pots then. We used a boring bracc to put holes in the wood bottom and into these we put canes—generally hazel cut from the woods—as ribs, which were then covered by net which we made from a big ball of tarred twine.

'The pots were on long ropes with corks two fathoms up and at spaces to the end. They were baited with mackerel and placed at the edge of the seaweed, where the fish oil would draw the lobsters out from their holes. When they entered the

Whelks gathered by Murdo on the Ullinish peninsula, Skye
(Photo: John Marchington)

pots they dropped down and couldn't get back out, though in those days we often had lobsters so big they couldn't get in! They just sat on the pots wondering how they could get the bait. So when we pulled in we had to keep a sharp eye for the big ones. You had to grab them while they were still in the water because as soon as you dried them they jumped into the sea.

'The fellow who came to buy the lobsters put them in boxes with sawdust in an old Ford car. He didn't come very often, and as we fished maybe for weeks we had to keep the lobsters in a huge box out by the shore—but not where the fresh water was runnin' because that would kill them. They're the tastiest thing you can get. The local laws said any lobster taken had to be over eight inches and we got 12/6d a dozen—any size. But we didn't bother with the crabs we caught and used to break them up because they took away the lobster baits. Nowadays even smaller crabs are fetching a great price.

'In those days you could get two caramels for a ha'penny and just 7/6d would buy a good pair of boots, with seven rows of tackets in the bottom to keep up with the wear and tear. A cap could be had for 9d and a plus-four suit for 35s. I never wore the kilt, but my brother did. I was afraid my legs would get too cold.'

Keeping warm has always been a priority in the gale-swept western isles, especially in those exceptional winters when the east wind blows for weeks on end. 'The worst was in 1947, when I had a big stackyard out there for the horses and cattle, as well as turnips for feed. I saw this great black over Barra so I thought I'd better get prepared for a long snow. It was on a Wednesday, and that night it started to thunder and lightning. By morning the snow was as high as the scullery wall. We were closed in for three weeks. But what a noise indoors when the snow started to melt. It sounded like a big river. When I looked up at the hills I thought: "If there's a quick thaw it'll be in the house", so I quickly dug a trench to let it run by.'

By then Murdo was already well into pony trekking, which became a main source of income for the forty years until he gave it up at the age of sixty-five. With the rapid improvements in transport, horseback holidays in beautiful, remote areas such as Skye soon became a major attraction. Ironically, the world which Murdo was never inclined to visit then had reason to come to him. 'The Americans came in crowds and sometimes people from as far as Guatemala were surprised to discover that they were not my first customers from their country. But even when I was very busy I was never tempted to work on Sunday. Then we always had a rest for the men as well as the horses.'

Much of Murdo's trekking was done around the beautiful island coastline, where occasional surprises lay in store. 'Sometimes we'd get the bodies of sailors washed up, and one day my neighbour Donald MacAlister found one which was well past its prime. He was frightened to death and I thought he was never going to stop running. But I made him go back and put his hand on the body because the old people used to say "Put your hand on a corpse and you'll never be frightened again". They were absolutely right.'

Murdo Macleod appears to have been born with that sixth sense which hovers in limbo between science and superstition. But is that so surprising for one whose long life on the outermost edge of society has embraced such contrasting generations? Some visitors might well regard his environment as harsh, one to retire from, but as soon as they see that impish grin and listen to the soft music of his voice they know that here is true happiness and contentment.

FROM THE ARCHIVES

Isle Of Mists

SKYE is the largest of the Hebrides, being above 60 miles long and of unequal breadth, so described by branches of the sea that there is not a place five miles from a good port. Its modern name is Norwegian from *ski*, a mist, which very well suits it. The rainy season lasts from August to the autumnal equinox. The number of inhabitants is 15,000, reduced 1750 by emigrations and poverty to 12 to 13,000. Their chief trade is black cattle and horses.

From William Camden's *Britannia* (1586, revised 1789)

Harbouring our Heritage

Leslie Hicks

NATIONAL TRUST HEAD WARDEN, CORNWALL

FEW people are as dedicated to their work as Leslie Hicks is. Indeed, he is so devoted to caring for the Cornish coast he takes only four or five days holiday each year. Reluctant to leave his isolated idyll, he accompanies his wife to Butlin's Minehead camp for the Christmas break—a very strange choice for one who prefers the cry of the seagull to the babble of children. He admits, 'It's my one concession to Martha'; but Mrs Hicks views it rather differently: 'I likes to know I'm still livin'. It's pretty quiet down here, you know.'

Even among Cornishmen, many of whom regard the simple act of crossing the Tamar as 'going abroad', Leslie's independence and loyalty are renowned: 'You'm never 'ome unless you'm in Cornwall'. But then he does draw considerable inspiration from living in and looking after the very area in which he grew up.

Leslie Roy Hicks was born on 8 March 1930, at the remote former port of Polruan on the south Cornish coast. 'Our cottage was right on the quay and the waves used to 'it the windows—that's why you can't ever get me away from the water. Us kids was just like limpets on a rock.

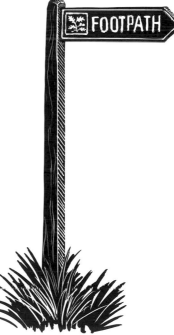

'Everybody was foreign then. We were so cut off that even the residents of Fowey—just across the water—called our village "Little Russia". In those days we couldn't so much as look at the girls from Fowey, and vice versa.'

Leslie's grandfather was born at Polruan, but left during the Depression to join the Grenadier Guards in London. When the family returned, Leslie's father had 'various jobs, mainly on Fowey docks, but also in Polruan boatyard during the war. At the docks they only got paid when there was work.

When a ship came in it was the first ones who rowed out to it got the jobs—mostly unloadin' coal and loadin' china clay, chiefly from St Austell. Today they get English clay from other parts but Cornish is twice the quality.'

In those days coastal villages as isolated as Polruan really relied on the sea for both transport and a living. 'There weren't many cars about then: if you saw more than one in a line it was always a funeral, or perhaps a weddin'. I can just remember a horse-drawn 'earse, and people who couldn't afford it 'ad to carry 'un—sometimes one-and-a-half miles from Polruan to Lanteglos church. Most of us didn't even 'ave the money for a bike. It were all downhill anyway. The policeman was the only one you saw on a bike.

'I didn't get a car until about 1954. It was an old Austin Ruby which had belonged to novelist Daphne du Maurier and still 'ad the petrol ration coupons in the front. A farmer bought it for twenty pounds and he gave it to me in return for shearin' his sheep in the evenin's at two shillings a fleece. I wish I still 'ad it.

'I don't much care for Daphne du Maurier's books—they are a bit fictionally for me and I was brought up not to say anythin' that's not true. Father wouldn't even go to the cinema because 'e said it was all fake.' But Leslie does agree that du Maurier, who was married in a church on his patch and often rented a cottage now in his care, did manage to capture the true spirit of the Cornish coast. However, this very romanticised corner of the kingdom could also be a very harsh place for impoverished natives.

'I was one of twelve children and we was very poor, though we always had somethin' to eat. We lived mainly on fish, rabbits and the spuds we grew. My gramfer on the other side, all 'e done was fish. You'd often go down and see a great big black shoal out to sea—that was pilchards or herrings. Then there was pollack and crabs and all sorts. It was all self-supportin' in those days, and you used to barter too. I still do. I 'ave four 'ens and a cockerel now and if someone 'as a few carrots they don't want, you give 'em a few eggs in return.'

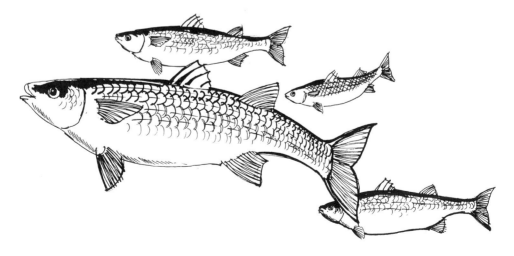

Mullet

Leslie attended Polruan school, where there were about seventy to eighty children in two classes. 'The biggest event I can recall was when the Germans decided to bomb us, at 5.18pm on 19 July 1940, just five minutes after the caretaker had left. The buildin' was almost flattened and we 'ad nowhere to go for seven weeks. There was a separate girls' school but no way were we allowed to join them.

'I wouldn't say I disliked school, but I was always involved in somethin' else. I never liked it indoors. Life was so much to do. A day is still not long enough: I don't like bein' governed by time.'

At the age of ten Leslie started to milk cows on a local smallholding. 'I took the cows to field before school and later on 'ad to clean out the cowshed. A chap could get a livin' out of just five or six animals then.

'Because we were really poor and it was 'ard and disciplined you made yer own fun. You'd just go and play allys (marbles), hopscotch or skippin'. That was the beauty of it—you just tired yerself out and went to bed. Weren't no vandalism then. It was all Sunday schools, too—mainly Methodist. The Wesleyan chapel's still goin' strong. I used to pump the organ there—gave it plenty of air so's the ol' chaps could raise their voices!'

Apart from earning 'a couple of shillin's a week' on the farm, schoolboy Leslie also did 'a few other little jobs—just survivin'. I was always expected to help manure the garden, bringin' up seaweed from the beach, mainly the flat weed (kelp), as well as a bit of sand. But we 'ad to get what we could, even any big fish which washed up—anythin' that'd rot down.

'There were lots of vegetable and flower shows then and father and my eldest brother were very keen. Sometimes we'd get a bit of dung if we 'elped with the 'arvest. No artificials then. 'Twas all your own skill with what you grew for the show. You'd never spend on the garden then, except perhaps a few seed potatoes. But if you was crafty you wouldn't even buy those. When someone else had theirs a year you bought a gallon from 'im and picked out some for seed.'

On leaving school at the age of fourteen, Leslie worked full-time on a smallholding, but there was no fixed pay. 'They gave 'e what they thought—about four shillings, and odd things like a drop of milk or cheap potatoes. They wouldn't *give* you a bag because they never 'ad a big livin', nor a lot to play with.'

Leslie's basic hours were about 8am to 5pm, 'but the cattle always came first and we was often late. You couldn't say, "I'll leave that drop in that cow for tomorrow" because if you did that they'd soon get bad with mastitis. The milk always 'ad to be right as there were four or five people sellin' it round about and anyone complainin' would soon change. But there was never no rush to go 'ome anyway because there was nowhere else to go after tea.'

Farming dominated Leslie's life for a long time. 'I worked for one man for eleven years. I lived with him and we was like father and son. There was a real bond between us, so when the chance of other work came up I gave him a full six weeks notice. This was in the early fifties, when I started part-time with the county council, and later the parish council, cuttin' footpaths—mostly on the coast.

'Then the National Trust bought some of the land and said, "Please look after it". I didn't get much money at first as there weren't many members then and they didn't 'ave much cash. Anyway, I wouldn't sting 'em as I always believed in the Trust itself—all I was doin' was supplementin' my farm income. I also used to shear sheep evenin's, and was always layin' lawns for people.

'Most of my Trust work's been involved with footpaths and tree plantin'. I'd never choose a job indoors. But it's changed a lot, and if I was startin' out I wouldn't look at it now because you're tied up in paperwork.'

But one thing Leslie has always enjoyed during over forty years (the first twenty years of those part-time) with the National Trust is meeting such a wide variety of people. And they come from all over the world to enjoy the magnificent Cornish coastline of his patch, which has forty miles of footpath, running from Lansallos in the east to Par in the west. Indeed, his fame has spread surprisingly far. For example, one day he passed two ladies along the coast path and heard one whisper to the other: ''Tis 'e'. So Leslie stopped and said: 'What do 'e want, my dear?' Then he discovered that they had seen his photograph in a magazine while flying across the Atlantic, and now they wanted his autograph.

Although he prefers the winter, when cold winds and often turbulent seas suit the craggy coastline but drive most visitors away, Leslie never resents anyone seeking solace in his coastal kingdom. Indeed, he is always willing to help, and in some cases come to the rescue. Take the time he was out cutting a path '. . . and an old lady came up, very distressed. She couldn't remember who she was and I decided there was no way I could leave her there so close to the cliff. Of course, I 'ad to leave my machine to summon help. First, I told her to 'ave faith in me. I said, "You must have relatives somewhere and I'm goin' to take you down in my Land Rover till we find them".

'Well, as luck would 'ave it we soon met this chap and 'e knew 'er. So 'e rode in the back with us to Fowey to the exact house, which was her daughter's. But there was nobody in, so we got a neighbour to look after her.

Pilot whale, one of the sea mammals Leslie has found beached in Cornwall

Allys (marbles) was a favourite game

'Three days later the phone rang and it was the lady calling to thank me. Turned out she'd been takin' tablets too strong for 'er, but now she was fully recovered. When I found her she'd already walked four or five miles and could easily have gone all the way to Plymouth, or even to her death.'

But by no means all visitors are welcome. 'In the mid-eighties this chap came down south after jumpin' bail from Liverpool Crown Court. What he'd do was go and get bed and breakfast for a night or two. Then he'd ask the landlady "What do I owe you?" But when she said, say, £30 he'd make out a cheque for £50, pretendin' it was a mistake so that she'd give him cash for the difference. Sometimes he'd even hire a car. He was a real con man.

31

Leslie has devoted much of his life to protecting the Cornish coast

'Eventually 'e got down this way and the police were closin' the net, at Polperro, where he was forced to abandon his car and went to live rough on the cliff.

'One day another chap came to see me and told me that he'd been out walkin' round Lantic Bay and seen a hole in the roof of the old smugglin' watch-house, which now belonged to the Trust but used to be rented by Daphne du Maurier. So I went to look, unlocked, and found that someone had been in and 'ad a good fry-up. By the way things was laid about I thought the intruder was comin' back and that there was a good chance it was the chap on the run. So I phoned the police and 'ad to show a keen young constable what 'ad happened. He went off duty at 10pm and they said they'd raid it at 1am with detectives and dogs. But the con man saw their lights comin' and went out on the rocks so's the dogs couldn't pick him up.

'Next day I rang the Trust about the 'ole in the watch-house roof. Then I found a sleepin' bag and blankets was missin' from the watch-house, so decided 'e wasn't comin' back. I told my boss I'd 'ave a good scout round the cliffs later on. So I went to Manpower Services and asked for the two fittest men they 'ad. 'Fore long two young chaps reported and turned out they was rugby players—just what I wanted!

'We looked in every crack nearly 'alfway to Polperro, but there was no sign of 'im. I thought there was only one place left to go—a fishin' hut built with driftwood in the side of the cliff, which nobody would know was there. So off we went.

'After a bit a man comes along the cliff path towards us, but I'd only seen a poor picture of 'im in the paper and I 'ad to be sure 'twas 'im. So I said to the lads, see if 'e looks behind when he passes, and 'e did. He picked up his pace, too.

'Then I went to the hut and there were the missin' things, so we followed 'im. But then the path split, so I went one way to cut him off as I didn't want to arrest 'im down among all the people. When I stopped 'im I told 'im my suspicions and said I was makin' a citizen's arrest on a charge of breakin' in at the watch-house. But I also said that 'e'd 'ave every chance to prove 'is innocence and if 'e wasn't guilty I'd give 'im the biggest apology. I said, "You sit there quietly while I go to phone", and the lads stayed there with 'im. Later he admitted everythin' and got eighteen months. Then the Trust presented me with a cartoon of it in appreciation.' A fair cop, but how unlucky for the con man that he should choose the patch of 'wilderness' so jealously guarded by Leslie Hicks.

Fortunately Leslie has never actually been attacked by anyone, though he has been threatened many times. 'In 1992 two chaps in a speedboat came in on the bay and put a tent up. I asked 'em to shift as it was against the rules, but they said it was too rough, which it was. So I said, "OK, but take the tent down by day so's not to encourage anyone else".

'Next day the wind had gone but they'd still made no effort to move. Then they said they couldn't move the boat, so I said I'd 'elp. Suddenly one went berserk and picked up this 'uge rock and threw it against the cliff face. So I said, "Right,

Turbulent seas suit the craggy Cornish coastline

I'll go and get the proper authorities". But they was underway before I was even up the top.

'Campers are the main problem, especially in Dormobiles which can get in most places. They like to be on their own in a quiet spot, but there's no overnight parkin' allowed here. They come out with all sorts of protests and excuses, such as "I've fought in the war". One chap I asked to move his vehicle even said "Come on, 'it me". But you've got to know when to walk away and hand it over to the police. And you must treat everyone the same—be firm but polite.'

Luckily, for every awkward visitor there are thousands who go away delighted by what Leslie protects and provides. Indeed, one person has been so pleased he has funded a special seat in Leslie's name. This is the first time the Trust has allowed such a memorial to carry a plaque bearing testimony to a staff member.

When Leslie saw a ship sail in a gale he knew she'd lose some deck cargo

Unfortunately, Leslie has never found anything really valuable on the beach, though he still dreams of stumbling across a keg of whisky. 'I'd roll it up into the bracken and hide it, and whenever I was down that way I'd 'ave a good ol' suck at it.'

However, Leslie has found many items of practical use in his job. 'I've always been a great believer in recycling, ever since us youngsters collected waste paper and tins durin' the war. And now I take all the bottles which people throw away to the bottle bank on Saturdays. I believe that if people don't see litter they won't leave any. Some years ago the Trust removed all its litter bins because they were unsightly and encouraged litter. The county council thought we were mad, but it's been a great success.

'I've never bought more than three metres of rope in all the years I've been a Trust warden, as so much of it washes ashore. And in the old days I always used driftwood to make stiles. In any case, there wasn't the money to buy timber. The Trust would say "Here's a pound of nails", and I'd get on with it.' But these were no botched constructions. On the contrary, one of Leslie's bosses always used to say, 'I likes those stiles better than they new ones. Them looks the part.'

Strictly speaking, any wreckage found along the shore is the property of the Crown, but as Leslie says, 'There is an unwritten law on finding. And only a Cornishman knows how to hide stuff. Many's the time I used to wait for a gale of wind, and when I saw a ship sail out from Fowey I knew darn well that she was goin' to lose some of her deck cargo. I'd look at the wind and work out where any wood might come in so that I'd be the first down there.'

But there have been the sad finds, too, such as the dead horses washed up, especially just after the war. 'We reckoned they were being exported for meat.' Then there have been beached basking sharks, pilot whales, dolphins and seabirds, some of them oiled. 'We haven't had any really major pollution incidents down 'ere, just the odd pumping out of bilges. There was one fairly big oil spill a few years back and I reported it, but I didn't panic and within six weeks you wouldn't 'ave known it was there. A lot of people do over-react to these situations and there's never that number of birds killed. When there was that big Shetland oil spill in 1993 I said to my wife, "I hope it stays rough—let the sea do its work. The tide and nature will cleanse it." And so it did. Nature will always have her way in the end. Sometimes the detergents they put on do more damage than the oil.'

Yet there have been many times when nature was distinctly unfriendly, such as in the bitter winter of 1962–3, 'when it was a job to keep the cattle alive. They say that's when Cornwall put her pipes underground.'

'But no matter what comes along, I've never been afraid of the sea. Whatever you put out there, it's all man-made and you've only yerself to blame if somethin' goes wrong. But I wouldn't ever go in a plane as you've no control over it. I did go in a helicopter once, at the Royal Cornwall Show, but that was only to accompany the grandchildren.

'I can't imagine livin' anywhere else. The coast is part of me—it's different all the time, with ships and clouds passin' and all the birds such as the gannets divin' for fish.

'Times used to be tough down 'ere all right, but given the choice we'd always go back to them old "bucket and chuck it" days. It didn't matter that we 'ad to get the water from a spring in bull's meadow, that our best entertainment came from a wind-up gramophone, and often all we 'ad was driftwood to burn on the black lead stove. There was always respect, and that's somethin' we've never forgotten down 'ere—if you lose that you'm as well dead. Whenever I'm out in the Land Rover, I always take care to look at and acknowledge people passing.

'Nowadays people often spend what they 'aven't got, but we would never borrow if there was no money to buy meat before next pay day. Anyway, with hens in the yard and spuds in the ground there was always egg and chips.'

Unlike the new breed of warden, men who have studied sciences such as ecology much more than they have considered the foibles of Man, Leslie has a very practical approach to conservation. He might resent all the paperwork and humbug which increasingly conspire to keep him from his precious coast, but his wisdom is that of the ages. While others believe that they have introduced new management techniques, such as grazing headlands to encourage wildlife, he knows that they are only going back to what he knew as a boy. 'It's gone full circle really, but now they rely on textbooks where we went by instinct.'

However, there is at least one man out there striving to blend the best of old and new. Leslie's son Geoffrey, who was well trained by his father, now wardens neighbouring Trust land at Lansallos.

Against this background, it was not surprising that the National Trust chose Leslie to represent Cornwall at the re-launch of Enterprise Neptune. 'It was the biggest honour I've ever 'ad. They could 'ave sent anyone who's been to college and learnt to speak, but they chose me, someone who wants to retain the dialect.'

But even stronger than Leslie's love of the language is his passion for the sea and coast. And there is no doubt that this will remain foremost in his mind for when I spoke to him in his workshop office there were half-a-dozen fishing rods on the side. 'They're all ready for my retirement', he said with a pixie's twinkle in his eye. But did I detect just a touch of salt already on the rod rings?

FROM THE ARCHIVES

Sea Fever

EXPOSED to the fury of the winds, one marvels at our modern craze for the sea; not merely to come and gaze upon and listen to it, to renew our youth in its salt, exhilarating water and to lie in delicious idleness on the warm shingle or mossy cliff; but to be always, for days and weeks and even for months, at all hours, in all weathers, close to it, with its murmur, 'as of one in pain', for ever in our ears. Undoubtedly it is an unnatural, a diseased want in us, the result of a life too confined and artificial in close, dirty, over-crowded cities. It is to satisfy this craving that towns have sprung up everywhere on our coasts and extended their ugly fronts for miles and leagues, with their tens of thousands of windows from which the city-sickened wretches may gaze and gaze and listen and feed their sick souls with the ocean. That is to say, during their indoor hours; at other times they walk or sit or lie as close as they can to it, following the water as it ebbs and reluctantly retiring before it when it returns. It was not so formerly, before the discovery was made that the sea could cure us. Probably our great-grandfathers didn't even know they were sick; at all events, those who had to live in the vicinity of the sea were satisfied to be a little distance from it, out of sight of its grey desolation. This may be seen anywhere on our coasts; excepting the seaports and fishing settlements, the towns and villages are almost always some distance from the sea, often in a hollow or at all events screened by rising ground and woods from it. The modern seaside place has, in most cases, its old town or village not far away, but quite as near as the healthy ancients wished to be.

From W. H. Hudson's *Afoot In England* (1909)

LAST OF THE MUD 'SKIPPERS'

BRENDAN SELLICK AND TONY BREWER

MUDFISHERMEN OF BRIDGWATER BAY

Tony Brewer

Brendan Sellick

WHEREAS most fishermen use boats to lay their nets, Somerset's Brendan Sellick and Tony Brewer are captains of archaic mud-horses which look as if they come from the Heath Robinson stable. The reason is simple: these men work in a sea of mud rather than one of water, and with over at least five centuries in the business, local families have found no better way to skip across the ooze in the race against the tide. But in recent years much has changed, the sea is not the provider it once was, and it seems likely that no one will follow in the glutinous footsteps of these two mud-horsemen of Bridgwater Bay.

For Brendan William John Sellick there was never any question as to which path he would take. An only child born on 20 November 1934 into a world of mud and fish, he squelched along behind father almost as soon as he could walk. 'Grandfather and Great-grandfather were mud-fishermen too, though originally Great-grandad was a stonemason from Nether Stowey and came down here when a girl told him he could make more money in fishin'.'

At first the family lived in Bridgwater and used to travel by pony and trap out to the nearby coastal hamlet of Stolford, that traditional centre of mudmen where Brendan was to grow up in an old fish cottage. He has lived at Stolford ever since, but now has a modern bungalow.

'To begin with there was half-a-dozen families makin' a livin' out of it. Good catches used to be taken by pony straight into Bridgwater market, but a lot was also sold door to door. There were no fridges then, and a woman would always go round with the fish straightaway.

'It was a tough life and almost everybody was poor then, but I suppose we was middle-rated, a bit better off than a farm worker. After the pony, my father had a little Austin 7, then an Austin 12.'

Brendan was one of about 150 children at Stogursey school 'which was four miles away, and I had to walk the first mile before catchin' the school bus. It was

OK, but I was always glad when it was high days and holidays so we could go out rabbitin' and fishin'. And Father used to take me down under the rocks to shoot ducks. There were lots of people out with guns then. Not many now though—they all want to take photographs instead.

'Rabbitin' was great fun, and very important when food was so scarce. Us schoolkids used to go behind the harvester stitchin' the corn, eventually ending up with a small uncut patch which had all the rabbits in. We'd surround this—there was always a good turnout—and knock 'em on the head with a stick or stone when they ran out. Bill Woods used to come out in his invalid carriage and swipe 'em with his sticks, but once he missed and fell over backwards so he couldn't move. Us kids laughed like hell. Bill used to like a drink and sometimes ended up in the ditch, where he used to keep his hand on the hooter to let people know he was there.

'Another great character I remember from schooldays was Tony Brewer's grandfather, Johnny King. He said he was in the last of the old sailing ships, and we used to call him Black Bob.

'When I was five, Father had a ninety-some-odd-pound sturgeon in his net. He brought it back over his shoulder, still alive and breathin'. He wanted me and Tony to sit on it for a photo, but I was screamin' because I was scared of it, so I didn't. As the sturgeon was declared a royal fish, Father had to offer it to the Crown, but they didn't want it so it was sold to a fishmonger at Weston-super-Mare.

The 90lb sturgeon which Brendan's father netted in 1939

'Another time Father brought back a little seal. It was in his net and he knocked it down and killed it with a stone, but he always regretted it after.'

So when, at the age of fourteen, Brendan left school to work with his father he was already well versed in the rigours of outdoor work and the ways of nature. 'But I had no wage to start—Father just gave me a bit of money when I wanted it. I'd already helped him a lot while at school, but full-time it was very hard. When I look back I think nobody would do it now. Even I don't work like I did then.'

Yet young Sellick still found time for at least a little fun, sometimes with unforeseen consequences. 'Once when I dived in the sea I hit my head on a rock and the current was so strong I thought I was going to drown. But I survived, as I did the three times I came off a friend's motorbike, even when I went over my chum's shoulders like a rocket.

'To be safe, you've always got to respect the tide. Two blokes—father and son—drowned out here only last year (1991). It was a lovely mornin' and they came over from Burnham in their boat. We'd seen them dozens of times before. Nobody knowed what 'appened. They found 'em about a week later all tangled

Off to work in the old days: Brendan's father, Bill (right) and Herbie Chilcot

in their nets. Out there in places the current is so vicious you can 'ardly stand up in a foot of water.

'Another time Fred Brewer panicked when he was out fishin' with his mud-horse. It was dark and foggy and he became exhausted. Luckily when he called out for help I heard him, so Father and me went down to pull 'im out.'

Fortunately, Brendan learned well from his father and has never been cut off by the tide or trapped in the once-deep mud. Today, for some unknown reason, much of the mud—'thousands of acres'—has been scoured away. 'Much of it used to be about fifteen feet deep, but now it's gone down almost to the peat bottom. I think the power station has altered the current. Hinckley Point is like a great mountain stuck out there and I'm sure that's shifted the wind. Since it was built, millions of tons of mud have gone. Sometimes, when the wind goes back south, you'll get tons and tons of sediment come in, but it soon goes out again. In the old days it was impossible to go out without a mud-horse.'

The design of the mud-sled has scarcely changed over the centuries, though the 7ft long, 18in wide bottom board is now made from different wood. Tony Brewer told me: 'The old people always used an elm coffin board from the local undertaker, but when they couldn't get these in the war years they went over to pirhana pine, and we've stuck to it.

'It's about a day's work to make a "slid". The only bit that really wears is the bottom board, which becomes wafer-thin after twelve to eighteen months.' Because of this, the mudmen always have a spare at hand, and have had to make quite a few over the years because sometimes they are washed away in storms. Traditionally they are weighted down with large stones and left on the shore, but even the heaviest rocks are no insurance against nature's worst onslaughts.

Brown shrimps

Once Brendan tried a Swedish snow vehicle, 'but the salt kept fouling the works and it was far too expensive to keep up. It took me a whole season to pay it off.'

Today, all costs must bear close scrutiny as the catches have declined so. 'Nowadays it's so unpredictable and we rely on a bit of all sorts, including cod [best catches December–January], Dover sole, skate and eels. Thirty years ago the brown shrimp was the main thing, but now it's only about ten per cent of the catch and we have to get a lot more fish. The shrimp is caught all year round, but mostly from August to November. We blame the power station for the loss of shrimps—it sucks in enormous amounts of water, and when the water comes out everything in it is cooked. They tell me the whole channel goes through the station once every four years. It's all the little offspring, the eggs and stuff, which really suffer. They get sucked in and killed much more easily than the adults.'

Brendan took me mud-fishing on a cold, blustery day in November, though while he pushed the sled across the glistening ooze I followed his son along the relative safety of the firmer-bottomed creeks. 'Riding' a mud-horse is certainly no job for the faint-hearted, for a good shove is required to get it going and there are numerous creeks to negotiate. But once Brendan got the revs up with his almost mechanical legs, the beast developed quite a speed across the open plains.

The nets are about a mile to a mile-and-a-half out and can only be attended when the tide is low enough. 'We don't usually go out at night now as you don't get half the stock and it doesn't pay. We generally go out about two hours before low tide and can stay out for as long as three-and-a-half hours. We certainly need all the time there is, with maintaining the nets as well as emptying them. There's always a lot of weed about, and a terrible lot of rubbish in the summer. We 'ad a cod with a plastic cup in its stomach once. Some fish even have elastic bands on their heads, and there's always lots of crisp packets as well as bits of sanitary towel.'

This is often cold work too, 'with hailstones like needles goin' in your face. In February it can be very icy, and when I was a boy you never had the clothes you get now. We never 'ad a wellington boot, and in any case they'd 'ave been no use. We wore shorts and ladies' tights. Tony even used to go out in shorts when it was freezin'. Sometimes you could cry with the pain in your feet.

Conger eel

'Early '63 was the worst I can remember. Everything froze up and we lost any amount of gear because when the tide went back it took it with it, snarled up in the ice. But 1947 was very bad, too—Father went out shooting a lot of ducks, and we almost lived on them. Nobody could get much food then, as it was all on ration. We used to eat peewees [peewits], curlews, plovers, the lot. Our favourite was the peewee. Dad used to get about a dozen of 'em—gorgeous: just cook 'em like a chicken with a bit of bacon on. But in those days a bloomin' pheasant was like havin' a Christmas box. Now they can't give 'em away.'

Even Brendan's quiet backwater had its share of excitement during the war years. 'In 1939 everyone in the south was on alert for the invasion, and we had a battalion of troops here from Blackpool. This little road out here was full of trucks. Anyway, the day the soldiers arrived they sent sixty out on the beach for an exercise. When they got down there they saw Fred and Jack Brewer and my father coming back up the mud with their sledges. Well, you can imagine, they thought they was spies and three soldiers went down to arrest them. After they realised their mistake the officer apologised, but the most frightening thing was that he admitted he had nearly given the order to open fire. You have to remember that everyone was hyped up then. Lord Haw Haw on the radio put the jippers up everybody. But our fishin' was only stopped for twelve months after the near-shooting. The Army wanted the bay for exercise.

'The soldiers first put their tents up, and then the cookhouse. Later the Yanks came, and most asked: "Got any sisters?" One of them was the boxer Joe Louis, who was a sergeant in the Marines.

'Father had TB and was not called up. Cor, we used to find some stuff on the beaches then. I always remember one drum Dad picked up—it was all rusty on the outside, but he said: 'Nothing wrong with that, you!' And he was right. Inside it was still clean as a new pin and contained twenty-eight pounds of dripping! We ate every bit.

'We also had lots of string—that was a great scarcity then—from all the parachutes. And we got the big material targets the bombers used to drag behind. Some people made curtains from 'em.'

But coastal folk have always been great beachcombers and sometimes whole communities have received real windfalls. One notable occasion happened at Stolford in about 1910, during the time of Brendan's grandfather. 'A coal ship, the *Secret*, got right in under the rocks and the skipper could hardly do anything about it as he had only a cabin boy with him. So in order to save his ship, he said to the villagers that they could 'ave all the coal if they took it off. So they did, and each 'ouse 'ad a bloody great 'eap which lasted for years. But when the lord of the manor came down with his 'orse and cart the skipper wouldn't let him have any!'

Today there are no wrecks on this beach, which is just as well, as Bridgwater Bay is a National Nature Reserve. Beneath the ugly backdrop of the power station only long lines of fishing nets—totalling a mile or so in length—straddle the great expanse of mud below Stolford. Remarkably, their position has remained unchanged since Grandfather Sellick's day. 'The old people soon found the best places and there's been no need to change. Once or twice I've experimented with different angles and spots, but without success.'

There are two main types of net here: the upright gill-nets which ensnare passing fish such as cod, and the funnel-shaped shrimp nets, once called 'hoses', which trap mostly smaller fish such as sprats as well as the shrimps. In addition Brendan has scattered, low-slung, baited eel nets.

'In the old days we used to take the twine and cotton nets in once a fortnight to preserve them in Zulu clutch, a treacly stuff which we used to melt down in a big ol' copper that we lit. Then they all 'ad to be dried carefully. There's no

doubt the introduction of nylon nets in the early sixties saved us an awful lot of work.' However, the wooden stakes—ideally elm—which are used to support the nets, last for fifteen years or so in the mud and salt water without any special treatment.

As I watched Brendan empty his nets he cursed the amount of weed which they trapped: 'Just look at this mess—it's all those bloody winds we've been having for a week or two. But there's no better way of doin' this. You could build whatever you like out here for strongness, but you get one wild night and the whole bloody lot's gone. It's so unpredictable. You're out here one night and you get a good catch and you think this is bloody good, but then next day everythin's disappeared.'

Brendan described the day of my visit as a lean one, with only a few pounds of sprats and shrimps, although we did return with half a dozen eels and about seventy pounds of small cod. 'In past years we had so many sprats you couldn't carry 'em in. Ideally what I like is about a hundredweight. On a good day we can get about thirty to forty pounds of

Brendan emptying shrimp nets in 1992

shrimps, and we've had two hundredweight of eel on a tide. About a fortnight ago I had some hundred cod totalling 350 pounds, but that was my best day for years and you really do need consistent catches to make a livin' at it.'

Today Brendan continues to sell his fish directly to the public as well as to fishmongers. 'A lot of eels go to the Continent, and sometimes I take 'em down to London. They fetch a good price there—always alive, of course. Eel's my favourite supper—stewed, with parsley and onion, and a bottle of wine or rough cider.

'In the summer we sometimes get big conger eels round 'ere, and they tear the nets up a bit. A few get in the shrimp nets—it's an easy feed for 'em. We 'ad one of fifty pounds the other day, but once we 'ad one of ninety-six pounds washed up on the beach. At one time there were a lot about and we think they were stunned by Navy exercises. They go in the net after the trapped little fish, 'ave a belly full and sleep it off. They can get out easily and think they're safe in there— which they are when the tide's up, but when it goes back they're stranded. With a big one you can see its tail hanging out the end of the net, which sags down on the mud with all the weight.

'My biggest cod have been 25 to 30lb, and in 1975 I had a 19½lb brill, which was then over two pounds heavier than the rod-caught record. Bass makes a good price—over £6 a pound in the shops now, though we see only half that. When I was a kid it fetched a shilling a pound, so when I caught a fifteen-pounder I thought I 'ad a fortune. That's about my biggest.'

Ironically, one of Brendan's long-standing customers is the power station. 'All these years they've tested the fish once a month and they've never found anything wrong with 'em. They always take a dozen pound of plaice and a dozen pound of shrimps. But the county council at Taunton make their own occasional checks, too.'

Now that so much of the mud has gone from the shore, Brendan is able to drive a tractor part-way out to the nets, but negotiating the creeks and boggy bits calls for great care. The tractor is one of the few aids which this tough little man has taken on board in later life. When you look at him now, treading the mud for all he's worth, you get the impression that this character who has appeared on Blue Peter, Keith Floyd's cookery programme and other TV shows could go on for ever. But sadly it seems as if his way of life will not, because his son and son-in-law, albeit willing to help out while no other work is available, cannot see a real future in it.

Tony Brewer comes from the only other family retaining the ancient rights to set stakes for nets in this protected area, four miles from the mouth of the River

Parrett, with Burnham-on-Sea to the east, Hinckley Point power station to the west and Steepholm Island to the north. But sadly, illness has prevented Tony from working the tides for over three years now. 'And I don't half miss it.'

Records at Stogursey church reveal that the Brewers have been Stolford fishermen for over 500 years. However, Tony was born in South Wales, on 17 August 1932, because his father was then temporarily a miner. 'Now it looks as if I'm the last because my son has a disability which prevents him from taking it on. Also, it's not a job that you can do part-time because the nets must be attended regularly.'

When he was only eleven, Tony started to help his father at Stolford. 'After school I had to clean the fish and go off on my bike to sell it. In those days if people wasn't home you could go in and leave the fish: you always knew just where to put it. And you always had your money next time you called. It's different now, with nearly all "foreigners" moved into the district.'

On that school round Tony sold Dover sole for a shilling a pound, Stolford dabs (flounders) for 8d a pound, skates for two shillings each ('just with the belly taken out then'), and shrimps for sixpence a pint. 'But when we got a car in 1950 we were able to take a set of scales with us for weighing, so the pints soon disappeared.'

'We were just walkin' back when this Spitfire turned on us . . .'

(Left) *Stolford fisherfolk: Granny (Lizzy) and Grandad Brewer in about 1890; (right) Tony empties his nets*

On leaving school Tony worked full-time for his father. 'At first I had no wage, but on a Saturday night, on the way back from delivering to Combwich, I was allowed to keep all the threepenny bits—silver as well as cornered ones.'

The war years and just after certainly brought plenty of excitement for the Brewer family. Not only was there the occasion already mentioned, when the Army nearly opened fire on Fred and Jack Brewer and Bill Sellick, but another when Tony and his father were actually attacked by the RAF! 'It was in 1948, when I was sixteen. We were just walkin' back across the mud when this Spitfire came up the bay and had a go at some gulls. Then he turned on us and a burst of canon fire went between the sledge and me. Luckily he missed, and before he could have another go the airmen on the nearby range fired some red Very lights to warn him off. I don't know what happened about that incident, but I do remember that if it happened again we had to try and get the number of the aircraft!'

Many hazards remained even after the military left the area. 'Once I found some 1,500lb, semi-armour-piercing bombs which had been offloaded but hadn't gone off. They were only a hundred yards from my nets and I must have gone over them loads of time. I only discovered them years after they'd been dropped, when the mud had been washed away.

'Also, in 1969 I found six 1,200lb aerial depth charges about half a mile from my nets. The Navy blew five of them up in the water, but one was exploded on

The mud sledge—unchanged for centuries. Hinckley Point power station is in the background

the mud and broke windows as far away as Burnham. They think the Germans dropped them because they thought they saw a periscope below.

'Another exciting episode happened when I went out for a pee one night. I heard this cry in the distance and called Dad. He said: "That's Uncle Fred", and so it was. The nose had broken off his sledge and we had to go out to help him.'

After National Service, Tony returned to the fishing life and eventually received a helping hand when he married Eirwen, who, among many other chores, used to deliver fish to houses in nearby villages. She says: 'One customer couldn't pronounce my Welsh name so he always called me Joan. Today everything is so different, but at least when we visit our local church we know everybody. It's a little wooden building which originated in the Fens, and we only get eight to twelve people attending the services, twice a month.'

The Brewers, too, have been saddened to see catches decline in recent decades. They also point out that the power station has put local people off buying fish, 'especially whenever there's a radiation scare on the news'.

Like Brendan's, Tony's nets have always been in much the same positions— 'Even if you twist 'em a bit, they won't catch'. Because of this, the different rafts of nets have gradually acquired special names, including '14 Raft', 'Long Raft', 'Herbie's Ground' and 'Father's Seven'.

The licence for driving stakes in, originally issued by local landowner Lord Clifford but now by English Nature, allows the taking of any fish except salmon

'Carrion crows can be trouble with the trammel'

and sea-trout. 'But they're usually at the wrong level anyway. They think more of a bloody salmon nowadays than a bloke earning his livin'. On top of that all these new hygiene regulations are killing the fishin' off. It's a tough thing to be in now.'

Tony proudly recalls that 'everything I brought in was saleable. I always riddled the shrimps on the spot as soon as the tide cleared so that the young ones, and many of the unwanted fish in the nets, had a good chance of living.

'You could say my "biggest" catch was a very small fish—a sprat weighing 2oz, which is good for that species, but I've had a conger of 50lb in the nets. Once I caught a 5½lb Dover sole, and my best bass was one of 18lb 2oz on a line of hooks baited with "rot-gut" whiting—fish caught on the last tide and dead twelve

Snipe

hours. It must have been a long time ago, because I only got 1/6d a pound for it. And way before my time, in 1912, there was a bottle-nosed whale washed up at Stolford.'

But many creatures other than Man are interested in such rich sea fare. When I was out with Brendan a few turnstones pecked at the full nets ahead of us, less than twenty yards away as we worked along the line. 'They'm after the shrimps', he said. 'It's easy pickin' for 'em. They'm all around me sometimes.'

While these attractive waders are tolerated, other predators are not. As Tony told me, 'Gulls do most of the damage. Brendan and me are the only two people still allowed to carry a gun in the nature reserve. It's so that we can kill a few seagulls and scare 'em off. But there's hardly the need now, as when the bird

Hinckley Point power station

sanctuary moved in most of the birds moved out, especially the shelducks and gulls. Some of the gulls have been killed by botulism with so much rubbish around to feed on.

'When there were a lot of gulls we often used to see them come into the nets at night, when the moonlight reflected on the sprats, but if I hung a couple of dead birds in the nets that would keep 'em away for a while.

'Gulls are the worst enemy with the shrimp nets, but carrion crows can be trouble with the trammel and gill-nets as they can't alight on the water. Crows nearly always go for the gut, but sometimes they fly off with a whole fish, which they often drop when mobbed by the gulls.

'Also, since the mid-1970s we've had a lot of trouble with foxes taking fish in the nets. They like to chew the heads of mullet, and make a hell of a mess. Once I 'ad fifty pounds of mullet like it. Mind you, if you 'ave one, it tastes a lot better than one *I've* chopped the head off.'

Today Tony can only sit and reflect on the way of life which he has enjoyed for so long, despite the hardships and unrelenting weather. Of course there were uncomfortable days of thunder and lightning, 'when it rained so hard the mud was like water'; and times of intense cold 'when great blocks of ice smashed up the nets'—but there were also many fine catches and days of hot summer sun, when sea breezes cooled as no others can.

The outbuildings of Tony's coastal cottage remain full of the trappings of yesteryear, especially the nets which served him so well. 'We used to make our own on the kitchen table. It was mainly the men, and it took about seventy-two hours to knit one 6ft by 4ft 6in.' But now these many yards of nets of all ages catch spiders rather than fish, and the huge wooden 'mole' made specially by his father to knock stakes into the mud is but a dusty curio in the corner. Even the strong baskets which once carried over 150lb of fish about a man's shoulders are now mere repositories of other cast-offs.

Yet Tony remains entrenched in this small coastal community, and I cannot see him leaving it voluntarily. Proudly he relates: 'The last time this house changed hands for money was for £80 in about 1910'. It's certainly not easy to flush five centuries of saltwater from the Brewer blood, and so it's no wonder that Tony often just happens to appear for a pound or two of cod when Brendan comes back up the lane with his catch. Even the cats in the Brewer household refuse to eat frozen fish!

But sadly, it seems that before very long the Sellick mud-horse too will be put out to grass and then the Stolford flats will be left to the birds. The last of the mud 'skippers' will be gone for ever.

FROM THE ARCHIVES

Abundant Prawns

WHEN we come to the common brown shrimp and the prawn we observe a wonderfully close resemblance to the lobsters and crayfishes—so close, indeed, that a general description of any one of them serves almost equally well for the others. The prawn, so abundant on the south coast, is caught in large numbers while young, and sold as shrimps; the older ones are often considered as belonging to quite a distinct species. It may be observed that the prawn is armed in front with a toothed beak—a feature not possessed by the shrimp: also that the shrimp does not turn red when boiled.

From W. Furneaux's *The Outdoor World* (1905)

IN THE FOOTSTEPS OF MONKS

DICK DALLEY

SWANKEEPER AND DECOYMAN OF DORSET

IN the fourteenth century, when fresh meat was hard to come by in winter, monks at Abbotsbury kept swans to nourish the body rather than the soul. Today, deputy swanherd and decoyman Dick Dalley helps care for the birds— but now that meat comes ready-frozen, the swans satisfy man's spiritual rather than gastronomic needs. In 1993 pretty pictures of swans on postage stamps commemorated the 600th anniversary of swankeeping on Dorset's coast, but they told us nothing of the earthy character behind the scenes.

Christened Anthony Walter, Dick was popularly named after the fictional character Dick Barton—'special agent'. He was born on 12 May 1936 at Chickerel, near Weymouth, where his father was head porter at the hospital.

Dick's earliest memories of the Dorset coast concern the strong military presence necessitated by the war. 'They did a lot of bombing practice in these parts and experimented with the ol' Barnes Wallis bouncin' bomb—they retrieved one recently. And there was machine gunnin' of all sorts. Pilots used to come down and fire at silhouettes on the beach, so there were no cygnets hatched at the swannery.'

After leaving the local school at fifteen, Dick trained as a painter and decorator before 'working in a fruit shop and hauling fruit lorries'. But he was always interested in the outdoors, and it was through fishing for mackerel off the Chesil Bank that he met his wife, who came from an old Abbotsbury fishing family. In 1961 he started working for the Fox Strangways family, who bought the manor of Abbotsbury and Chesil Bank in 1543 and were granted the right to keep the swan herd by Henry VIII. 'Funny thing is, all that time back at school the careers officer told me about a job at the swannery. But I didn't apply then because I wouldn't go into lodgin's.'

At first Dick and his family lived at the idyllically situated but remote Cloud's Hill Cottage, owned by the Strangways estate. 'In 1963 we were cut off for six weeks. The snow was like white cliffs and bread came into the village by helicopter. It was a job to walk on Chesil Beach, the pebbles was frozen so 'ard.'

This was certainly a very tough time for the mute swans, which are particularly susceptible to severe winters. Dick recalls: 'When the ice lifted with the tide a lot of their food—mainly the eelgrass *Zostera*—was ripped out and lost, so many birds starved. It was nothing to get twenty to thirty dead in one day; I counted up to 250 bodies and then gave up. But at least bits of the Fleet never froze because they're fed by underground springs.' The swannery adjoins the Fleet, a saltwater lagoon nearly eight miles long, separated from the sea by the Chesil Bank and officially recognised as a wetland of international importance.

The Fox Strangways have long taken seriously their custodial role in guarding the birdlife of the Fleet, where as many as a thousand swans may be present in winter alongside large concentrations of ducks and rarer species. However, when Dick first started working for them he continued the long tradition of 'raisin' swans for the table. But I only ever reared 'alf a dozen. I used to feed 'em on kibbled maize, but later we changed to wheat as it 'as more protein.

'Lord Galway liked a cygnet, and sometimes he let one or two of the tenant farmers 'ave one. They were killed at five to six months old, when the meat was quite tender. Once there was a mix-up and Lord Galway was given one I'd kept aside because it was so thin. Anyway, 'e sent for me and said: "If I want a sparrow on the table I'll shoot one out of the French windows". Well, that was the last one I raised. But I liked Lord Galway—he was an honest man.'

Dick himself has eaten swan just once, many years ago. 'We wrapped this cygnet in foil and cooked it outside when we was burnin' some withies. It weren't too bad.'

Duck, too, were once an important part of the estate menu. Most were trapped by Britain's oldest working decoy, whose main pond was dug by hand in 1655. Originally, dogs called 'pipers' were kept to attract the ever-curious duck into five 'pipes' (long netting tunnels with a conical net at the end) over the water. Large numbers were caught in this way, but the practice was virtually redundant by the time Dick became decoyman. 'But we did still catch a brace apiece for each estate worker, and the big house used a few. Her ladyship specially liked to 'ave some teal.' Today, corn sweepings rather than dogs are used to attract wildfowl into the decoy, three pipes of which are maintained purely for ringing and research.

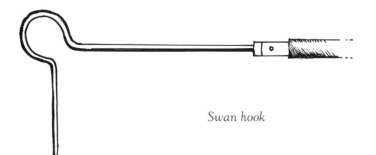

Swan hook

Eel trident

But whereas trapped duck receive only an alloy leg ring with a personal number, the swans also have the hive mark of the Earl of Ilchester cut into the web between the toes. The practice has continued since the sixteenth century, when many herds were protected by their distinguishing marks.

This 'branding' of swans is also still carried out under royal licence by the Dyers' and Vintners' Company, who once invited Dick to their annual 'swan-upping', when the birds are rounded up on the Thames. 'It was July 14, and they issued each boat with a bottle of rum "to keep the cold out". And later on I was given this "Vintners' tea", which turned out to be nothing more than a glass of neat Navy rum with a little bit of milk on top. It was a real booze-up. One chap got thrown overboard and 'ad to swim for it. We ended up at Sonning in this posh 'otel and 'e came in covered in muck and slime. We saw this bundle of rubbish on the floor and it suddenly got up—it was 'im! He very soon went out with a waiter on each arm.'

But not all old ceremonies are so riotous. At Abbotsbury, Dick's wife Betty still organises the delightful Garland Day, when local children gather flowers from the wild and from gardens. One garland is placed on the war memorial, but there is another which, with far greater tradition, is cast on the sea when the nets are hauled in, to appease the fish god. This is something very close to Dick's heart because he used to rely on fishing for part of his living.

'I used a trident and caught a lot of eels in winter when I was out of work, as there was no dole office. I used to put mine in a box—still alive, of course—and send 'em by rail up to Billingsgate through Weymouth station. Well, one day my mate went into Weymouth and the station master said: "Tell Mr Dalley I want to see him". It turned out that my box had broken and the eels had wriggled out all over the place. I never did go and see the station master, but I knew the eels got to Billingsgate safely as I 'ad the usual card back. The railway staff must 'ave gathered 'em up.'

Today Dick, who is also an auxiliary coastguard, spends most of his time looking after the swans and their wetland habitat. With swanherd John Fair and six other staff, he cares for a resident herd of some four to five hundred. 'Numbers haven't altered a lot in my time. They live an average of eleven to fifteen years and breed at three to four years. In 1992 we 'ad 103 pairs bred, most of 'em on five acres. A few odd ones nest away from the main area, but Mr Fox generally gets 'em. It's mostly the cygnets that's taken, but also some eggs and the odd adult swan. It's generally the weak birds lost—all natural control so

'I've seen the saddle-back take cygnets too'

nothin' to cry over. Even swans will turn on their own kind—it's built in 'em to push the weak or diseased ones away. And once out the herd they're easier victims for foxes.

'In the good ol' days the fox was easier to deal with because you could find a bird half-buried by one and put somethin' in it. You can't do that any more. But then we discovered that wooden eggs would put one off. We found teeth marks in 'em: 'e must 'ave thought 'is teeth was packin' up.'

Dick also had other predators to deal with. 'When the mink scare started visitors kept sayin' they saw them at Abbotsbury. Then one day this lady said she spotted one on the bank. I said: "I expect it's a water vole", but she said: "I don't think so because they're vegetarian and this one's eating a duck!" It turned out we had a family of nine mink. We accounted for seven, but the last two decided they wasn't welcome and moved to the top end of the village.

'I've seen the saddle-back [great black-backed gull] take cygnets too. There used to be a great big colony of terns along the beach here, and where they are you always get the black-back. They really started to take cygnets when most of the terns went and their food disappeared.

'One day a black-back got a cygnet and ate it alive right in front of everyone. So I went 'ome for me musket and that evenin', when all the visitors had gone, I shot the female. Then the male came straight down the barrel at me, but I got 'im too.

'You sometimes see the ol' saddle-back in the air with a duck nearby. Then suddenly there's only one bird there where the duck's been swallowed up.'

However, a healthy adult swan is far from helpless. Dick says a strong cob (male) can kill a fox. Humans are not entirely safe either, even experienced swanherds such as Dick. 'One day I was at the nest of a pair which had always done well and thought the cob there was protectin' his mate. But while I was reachin' down tryin' to catch the cob the real mate came chargin' in and hit me on the back of the head—probably with 'is wing. I was knocked right out, and when I came to there was four of the seven cygnets dead, crushed under me. But all I suffered was a stiff neck for a week or more.

'I've never 'ad a bone broken by a swan, but I've known people 'ave ribs and collar bones broken by 'em. And in the West Country once a girl was drowned when she was swimming by a nesting pair. I expect the cob clouted her. Sometimes cobs even kill their own cygnets accidentally when fightin' to protect them.'

Fortunately most of the visitors to the swannery are less aggressive. 'You get the odd incident, as everywhere, such as the time when someone pinched the decoyman's 'ead, from the dummy on display. I found it nearby when I hit it with a machine while cutting reed. Then there was the day when a load of students came down from Bourne- mouth and started throwin' shingle at the cygnets. They were foreign lads and the teacher with 'em didn't seem to 'ave any control. But after a while they went too far. One threw some mud at Mr Fair, and I can tell you they picked the wrong one there to throw a clod at!'

Many of the swans are as well travelled as the visitors. Recovery of ringed birds has shown that they often move considerable distances. Dick has had 'some come in from

In the winter of 1962–3 the bread came in by helicopter

March of progress: Dick now mows the Abbotsbury reeds, but in the old days they were cut by hand

sixty to seventy miles away. I always said they was commuters long before they built the railway. One of ours even ended up in Guernsey—quite knackered. But the people there clubbed together to buy it an airline ticket and John went to pick 'im up from the airport this side. But it's very difficult to get to know individual mute swans because they don't 'ave the different bill markin's like the Bewick's swans do.'

Dick Dalley is an occasional traveller too, visiting various organisations to give talks on his work. 'But we do get a fair number of over-enthusiastic helpers. Once one lady carried my slides in, tripped over and they went all over the place. Consequently they came up on the projector all upside down and out of order, so my talk to the beekeepers was chaos!'

Outdoors, things must be much better organised, including the regular burning and cutting of reedbeds to improve the habitat for wildlife and provide thatching material. But even such hard, physical work has its lighter moments, as Dick recalls. 'Two of us was out cuttin' reed and we stopped for breakfast. It was quite warm so I spread me sarnies out on the ground. Then I 'eard this swan comin' in over the reeds and 'e was so surprised to see us 'e dropped 'is load—right on me sandwich. I said to me mate: "I like sauce on it, but not that green gunge".'

Today, reed cutting at Abbotsbury is not so back-breaking, with a special machine like a glorified lawnmower to take the strain. However, the weather can still cause problems because the reed can only be cut and stacked dry and there are many wet days during the harvesting season, from January to March. 'Also starlings can be a pest when they break the reeds off at roost, and they always seem to pick the best. But we don't get the big flocks like we used to.'

A more unusual Abbotsbury harvest is swan quills. Each year Dick helps gather a few of the larger ones, which are used to make old-fashioned pens. Since the 1740s, Lloyd's of London have used these to record ships lost at sea in their Doom Book. Others are used to hold the hair on artists' brushes.

A live harvest, too, mixes freely with the swans, as pheasants reared for sport are often seen about the estate. In fact the marshland suits them well because the introduced pheasant originally came from a reeded, waterside, Asian habitat. Like all good countrymen who understand how well-organised shooting and conservation can work to mutual advantage, Dick used to help out with the beating on pheasant shoot days. But he was never keen on the special coot shoots which once took place at Abbotsbury.

'The 1904-built boat on display took three men—the Gun, his loader, and the rower. With men on the bank too, it was nothing for 'em to get rid of a thousand rounds in an hour. They used to say that the coots took the swans' food, but that's a load of rubbish, just an excuse for a shoot. There's no value in the coot. You might as well stick your boot in the oven.'

Unlike the decoyman whose cottage was half-demolished when a thirty-foot tidal wave swept over Chesil Bank in 1824, Dick now lives higher up, in the safety of the village. 'But we 'ad a good flood in December '89, when a lot of houses just along the coast were under water and we rowed out here all around the fields.'

The Dalleys and their seven children had to move when Cloud's Hill Cottage was gutted by fire caused by a generator fault. 'When I came back from takin' my daughter to church the place was well and truly alight. The boys were chuckin' buckets of water on it, but that weren't no good. They never rebuilt the place, but in any case it was lonely for my wife up there and she was very worried the time when we 'ad an escaped prisoner in the area: 'e came in a boat he'd pinched.'

But there is no doubt that Dick Dalley still follows a contented path in one of the most unspoilt parts of southern England, just as those monks did all those centuries ago. 'We get to meet people from all walks of life and the work varies with the seasons. Also, there's still quite a good community spirit. There's a lot of incomers in Abbotsbury, but most of 'em are nice people. Best of all, we've got both coast and countryside right on our doorstep.'

FROM THE ARCHIVES

Chesil Bank

HERE the coast winding much runs out into the sea. A bank called Chesil, composed of heaps of sand with a narrow channel between it and the land stretches along for nine miles. The south wind when it sets in breaks through this bank in many parts, and the north repairs it. By this bank, Portland, once an island, is joined to the land.

From William Camden's *Britannia* (1586, revised 1789)

PONY EXPRESS

ARCHIE MACDONALD

*HORSEBACK POSTMAN, FISHERMAN AND CROFTER
OF THE OUTER HEBRIDES
AND ESCAPED PRISONER OF WAR*

Resting the horse: postman Archie Macdonald in 1960

Aᴀʀᴄʜɪᴇ Macdonald is one of the last few men alive who once delivered Britain's mail by horseback. From 1954 to 1964 he rode to isolated dwellings among the maze of creeks and islands of North Uist, always trying to avoid being cut off by the tide. While mainland posties fretted over traffic jams, Archie pored over tide tables. Yet this was but one chapter in a most extraordinary life. Who could have imagined that the fourteen-year-old who went away to become herd boy on one of Britain's most remote groups of islands was destined to become a war hero.

Archie's roots are deep in the peat of the Outer Hebrides, but even in his late seventies he has not been one to vegetate. In 1992 he and his wife Catherine moved into the little Grimsay bungalow which they had built on land Archie once ploughed, their previous church manse having become too large and draughty for them. Now, from his picture window, he can view not only the house which his father built in the 1920s, but also the now dilapidated, once thatched one in which the family lived before that. Just behind them is one of the creeks which once formed part of Archie's 'highway', and beyond that lie the mystical, mist-shrouded hills which look unchanged since the day the British Isles rose from the sea.

Born on 11 August 1916, Archie had two brothers and six sisters. Like the majority of folk in the region, his father and grandfather were both crofters and fishermen, harvesting both land and sea to scratch a living. But his grandfather was also a church missionary, a most appropriate term in the days when visiting Britain's isolated communities was almost as adventurous as going into Africa. As Archie says, 'There was a long way between the congregations on all the islands where he held services. But he had plenty to do because it was all large families then and everybody went to church.'

Grimsay Public School, now closed, had two teachers and about thirty children. Archie liked it there. He was 'good at lessons but desperate to get out to work' because he was the eldest child in the family. 'It was all Gaelic spoken. Our schoolbooks were in Gaelic and we didn't even speak any English in the playground.

'Times were very tough and I used to run messages barefoot for mother while father was away at the lobster fishing all summer and early autumn. We lived on potatoes, fish and porridge. At one o'clock at school we got a cup of cocoa, but you had to bring a scone of your own.

'Father only came home at the weekends. Lobsters fetched 2/9d a pound and we made all our own pots. The catch went down alive in wooden boxes to Billingsgate. But the lobsters often died on the way in hot weather. If you got a bill with a mermaid on you knew straightaway that the fish were all rotten when they arrived in London.'

But Archie did not go straight into fishing when he left school. His first job was as 'herd boy on the Monach Isles, way out in the Atlantic, about ten miles west of Uist'. What an incredible adventure that must have been for a fourteen-year-old!

'Father heard about the job because this was one of his regular fishing haunts. He and the other fishermen had wee stone huts there and used to stay in them all summer. Some were thatched. There were three islands—Shilay and East and

Archie in the garden of his new croft in 1993. Behind him are (right) the croft built by his father in 1920 and (left) the remains of their earlier house

West. Shilay lighthouse was put out of commission when the war started and never lit again.

'On the islands there were seven families who all had cattle, together about a hundred head. At night I had to put them in an enclosure to keep them out the crops, and at 6.30am I let them out to graze. Then I put them back into the enclosure at 9am for the women to milk. At 10am I let them out again onto the machair grazing until 1pm, when I put them back into the enclosure so that I could get my dinner hour. At 2pm they were let out to graze until 8pm. I was out all day at it and glad to get to bed. I always slept in the same house there, but each croft had to take turn giving me meals, two days at a time.

'For the six months I was there I received £9 at the end, but at the start I was given a new oilskin coat because I had to be out in all sorts of weather. When the potatoes were gathered in and the corn secured in October they had no more need for me.

'The islands had their own missionary. He was allowed to keep one cow for milk for the family. As well as the crofters, most of the fishermen went to his services. They all had good strong voices in the Gaelic.

'Father then fished with his two brothers. It was all sailboats. The only one with engines was the twenty-four-foot mail packet. Father's boat had a jib and two mainsails, which became brown with all the dipping in kartkue. This came in lumps from the mainland ships' chandler and was melted in water in an old boiler with a fire under.

'There was a special big sailboat for the cattle, which took about four at a time to the sales, then held once or twice a year near Clachan. You can still see the remains of the wooden pens there. But the boat would only take one horse at a time—with the forelegs tied—because they were so strong.'

In later years, expansion of the ferry services was to transform life in the Western Isles, though the cost could be considerable for locals forced to make frequent trips. Not surprisingly, some had a few wrinkles. For example, Archie recalls how Donald Maclean would smuggle his Hillman Imp inside a big deep-freeze lorry when crossing from Lochmaddy to Uig, on Skye. 'He must have slipped the driver a few pounds.

'When I used to go across on the Kyleakin ferry, from Skye to the mainland, I noticed this farmer never used to pay anything. Eventually I asked him how this was and he said: "Oh, I'll be giving the man a good wedder", which is a castrated male sheep two or three years old and sometimes huge.'

After leaving the Monach Isles, Archie helped out on his family's croft, rented from the North Uist estate for about £2 15s a year. 'There wasn't a lot I could do there. We only had two cows and a few sheep. So after a year, when father bought his own boat, I went with him to the fishing for two seasons. The boat was built by Angus Stewart, here on Grimsay.

'If there was no wind we had to row to the fishing. In those days a big lot of lobster pots was five dozen, but we usually ran four dozen. Our bait was crab, mackerel and herring—really smelly stuff. You didn't have your own fishing patch—it was a free-for-all. We mostly went around the islands, and down round Lochmaddy later in the year.

'When the weather was rough a long rope with a dozen creels on was handier to lift than single-pot ropes. The longest rope was about fifteen fathoms, but nowadays they're much longer because there aren't the fish close in and the boats have to go away to the Atlantic deep water. But it's all so easy now, most men go out on big boats with diesel engines and many more creels, and everything comes ready-made—but we had to cut our own cork buoys from big sheets.

Archie became very attached to all three of his horses

'As well as the lobsters we caught lithe, which look like ling and would take your hand off if you're not careful, haddock, herring, mackerel, cod and dogfish, all mostly for our own food. If we had a lot we'd salt it for the winter. The herring was gutted, left whole and salted down in layers. Salt mackerel and new potatoes is the best diet you can get.'

But in the late 1930s fishing had to take a back seat when Archie took an opportunity to earn more money, in helping to tar the new roads. 'They were just rough gravel before. We stayed all week in a hut wherever the work was and came home on Saturday.'

By then Archie was well established in the Territorial Army, which he had joined at the age of sixteen. 'My first camp was in 1933, and I went every year till 1939, when I was called up into the Queen's Own Cameron Highlanders.

'I went to Inverness barracks for a month and was billeted at an old farm, under the command of Colonel Bailey of Dochfour, an ex-Great War officer. There were a whole lot of us there from Uist, Skye and Harris. Later we were at Fort George, where the discipline was terribly strict. A poor young chap called Rory was just walking along with his hands in his pockets when this big brute of an RSM came up and said "Come with me!". He took Rory straight to the tailor and had his pockets sewn up.

In 1939 Archie (left) was in the Military Police, along with John Mackintosh (centre) and (another) Archie Macdonald

'Later we were on military police duty guarding the Admiralty, 10 Downing Street and other buildings, and Churchill used to pass us nearly every day. But he always had his nose down reading the paper and didn't seem aware of us, so one time my chum didn't bother to salute him. Churchill only went a few paces and then came straight back to pull my mate up.

'After that we were at Aldershot and Bordon camp in Hampshire. I remember the day everybody polished up for the King. You always had a royal visit before going off to fight. That was their way of buttering people up. A week later we were sent over the Channel.

'We left from Southampton and arrived at Le Havre. Our whole division was captured on 12 June 1940, at the fishing village of St Valéry, while we were trying to hold Jerry back to let everyone get away from Dunkirk.

'Our major was an old veteran from World War I and he was in tears when he told us to fall in and throw our rifle bolts away so that the guns wouldn't be any use to the enemy. Then this young German searched me. He put his fingers into my breast pocket where I had this parcel from home, containing a razor and shaving cream which had burst when I dived on the ground. You should have seen the alarm on his face when he touched the cream, and then he smeared it all over me.

'As we set off to march to Germany I planned to escape as soon as possible. So the day after we left Tournai Barracks in Belgium Roderick Macisack and me queued up three times for bread to make sure we had enough rations, and they never noticed.

'A few miles on we were passing this field of corn, so about twelve of us broke out from the column to relieve ourselves, as we were allowed to. Then this great big Jerry sentry came along on his horse and in good English said: "Come on out. You've been in there long enough". So everyone got up, except the two of us. We lay there like mice, expecting a burst of fire to come in, but he just strode away. I can still see that Jerry's helmet above the top of the corn.

'We crawled across the field on our hands and knees and when we got out the other side there were two old Belgians waiting for us. We had quite a bit of French between us and after a while they went off and came back with a jug of coffee and a pile of sandwiches. But then they said "Allez". They wanted us to go.

'After that we spent two or three days in a big wood before starting to make for the coast at Calais. I was used to boats and with the good weather in June we thought we might be able to get back across the Channel. But when we got there Jerry was well dug in with barbed wire and when we touched it all these tin cans started rattling. Immediately they started blazing away, but they couldn't see us because it was dark and we were able to crawl back to safety.

'When we were near Béthune we were in a large orchard full of lovely apples, so we took as many as we could carry for future use. Unfortunately two gendarmes were watching and angrily arrested us. We kept talking to them in Gaelic and told them we were Dutch labourers. So they locked us in an unoccupied cottage and told us that they would take us to a Dutch farm next morning. But in the night we managed to loosen a small window and escape.

'After that we squatted in an empty cottage, but the neighbours noticed.

Luckily they were English naturalised Belgians and the two young girls there used to bring us food. They even gave us a clock. But after a few weeks they told us we had to leave, and so we went south.

'A farmer gave us civilian suits and we used to travel along the main roads carrying an old rake or shovel because we often had to pass Germans. But then this army motorbike and sidecar went by and two German soldiers with tommy-guns told us to stop. We thought we'd had it, but they spoke to us in broken French and we could understand them. They seemed to be looking for some village, which we didn't know, so we just answered them as best we could in French and told them to keep straight on. As soon as they roared away into the distance we bolted for the nearest cover and hadn't been in the trees long when we heard them coming back. They must have realised who we were. But by then we were well hidden and they soon disappeared. After that we kept to the side roads.

'Half of France was still free then and we hoped to reach it. When we did, we thought we were all set—but our troubles were only just beginning. The first thing Rory [Roderick] said was: "I'm going to steal a bicycle". His boots were so worn out he couldn't walk any more.

'Rory went into a café and asked for two bottles of English beer. As we walked away he picked up a bike. Then I started to take another, but as I glanced back I saw three men watching. So I shouted out to Rory in Gaelic: "Carry on, I'll catch you up in the next village". Then off I walked.

'When I got to the next village I couldn't find him at first, but then I saw him sitting in a café. He told me: "They were waiting for me here". So we had a few glasses of wine and went out, to where the mob were waiting: they tore into us. When they were kicking me my webbing burst so I grabbed it and started swinging. Rory was always spoiling for a fight anyway. I was well cut.

'Then the gendarmes came and took Rory away, but I managed to hide in a shed. Inside were half-a-dozen bikes, so I picked the best one and got away on my own.

'By the time I reached Marseille my money had just about run out, but I had a bottle of water. I told an old man at a nearby village port that I wanted to get to Africa and he said that there was a cargo boat leaving the next day. So I slept on the pier among the rubbish and the rats were over me all night.

'Next morning I was just going onto the gangway when two policemen came along and whisked me away to the barracks. But I couldn't have cared less because I was nearly finished with the hunger.

'After half-an-hour in the guard room this big black corporal came in and asked me if I was hungry. He returned with a bowl of broth and a loaf. It was a Foreign Legion barracks and they couldn't do enough for me. The sergeant used to take me down to the village at night and buy me a bottle of English beer out of his own pocket.

'Then I was taken in handcuffs on the train to Marseille, not to Lisbon as expected. There I joined about fifty others in the seamen's mission. I asked if anyone else there could speak Gaelic, and amazingly, there was a man from South Uist. I asked about Macisack and discovered that he was in hospital there, so I

'We attempted to escape by sea'

went up to see him and next day he was discharged. He told me that after I left he had been put in prison, but on the very first day he had just sauntered out while the guards were checking visitors' passports. I told him that someone had stolen my bike and that along the way I'd eaten a lot of grapes, but they gave me diarrhoea.

'At the mission there was an English captain who picked thirteen of us used to boats for an attempted escape by sea. He had arranged for a French fisherman to take us at night from Marseille docks out into the Mediterranean, where we were to be met by some British destroyer or corvette. We made the trip, but unfortunately the ship did not appear and the sea became very rough, so we were thankful to get back to Marseille for a while it had looked as if we would be lost at sea, after all we had survived.

'Eventually four of us managed to get away to the Pyrenees, but we had no guide and after four days we were hopelessly lost. We came across a couple of smugglers who gave us goats' milk, and then we hopped on a train to Madrid. But after only ten minutes two policemen in civvies came on and took out their revolvers.

'We were taken to the civilian prison at Barcelona, where we spent four months, ten to a cell. We were worse off than the poor fellows who went to Poland. The guards often used to leather us and hit us with a truncheon. Those Fascists were terrible and frequently shot prisoners. The conditions were foul. When they took us out for exercise there were always people sitting on the pavements delousing themselves. And we were made to work on the roads, carrying baskets of stones. But as soon as one road was finished it was abandoned and another started.

'Then, miraculously, one day the British embassy in Madrid sent a bus down and we were given new suits. After a week in a Madrid hotel we were bussed to

Gibraltar. As we went through the gate a Glaswegian in front of me spat in the face of the Spanish guard, who couldn't do anything because there was a big British guard on the other side. We got home on 17 October 1942.'

For his brave escape Archie was awarded the Military Medal. Modestly, he told me: 'I don't know why I was the only one of the four Macs who escaped to get the award. Perhaps it was because I was on my own the longest.'

After the war Archie went back on the roads labouring before going off to work for British Rail at Glasgow. Then it was back to Uist with a contractor laying the new road.

In 1954 Archie started work as a postman on £9 a week, which included an allowance of ten shillings three times a year for horseshoes. 'There were three of us posties in the area and we were all called Macdonald, though not closely related. We owned our own horses because we also did other work with them. Our uniform was a heavy, navy blue serge with a red stripe, as well as an overcoat, and a light suit for summer.

'At first all the post came by boat three times a week to the head office at Lochmaddy and was sorted out for the townships. A van brought it out to the sub-offices, from where we local postmen collected it. Soon after, airmail started to come in through Benbecula. An ordinary letter cost 2½d, but 2d if open.

'Some people got their mail early or late, according to the tide, and I was cut off once or twice. But most houses had a coble and then you could get off if you were prepared to leave the horse for later. When I had to go down the twelve miles to the smithy at Benbecula to get new horseshoes, I would be stuck there from 10am to 10pm waiting to get off again.

'One day I was out with an assistant when we got cut off. I was all right because my horse was steady enough for me to sit on while he swam across. Young Donald followed me and kept his legs up, but it was a waste of time because when his horse got into deep water it lunged forwards and he fell off.

'I did also use a boat for some deliveries. But one time I couldn't get into the bay with all the ice, so I went full ahead with the engine and there was such a crack I thought the boat was broken. Luckily it was all right.'

Willing as he was, Archie was not forced to go out in all weathers. 'In the very worst I left the horse at home. It would get very crabbed in the white weather. Also it would sometimes lay down, it was so tired with the weight of parcels on it. The butcher's meat was the worst. There were five shops on Grimsay then and I used to get their bacon and sausages by post, as well as butter, cheese, tea and sugar from merchants in Glasgow. I also carried boxes of turnips and carrots. You'd be going along nicely when all of a sudden there'd be carrots flyin' down the road where they were not packed properly.

The mail must get through! On Grimsay Archie had to negotiate many tidal fords

'One day my horse bolted when he was loaded with parcels and I was holdin' on for dear life. When he stopped the saddle was under his belly and half the parcels had burst.

'You'd be surprised at the things we had to carry then. One day a postie in the Western Isles was so disgusted with it all he threw the lot on the ground at the place where he took his rest. An old lady had ordered a poit leabaidh (chamber pot), which burst out of its wrapping and rolled down the brauch (slope). Some of the lads were watching him and in fits of laughter. They say that the same man used to drop half the junk mail in the peat bog.

'The weight limit for a parcel was 22lb, but this changed to 15lb. That made a great difference when there were ten to carry. I had a pouch on each side of the horse, a sidebag on my shoulder and a bag on my back. I remember when they were petitioning for the road a lady said: "The postman's out on an endurance test, not working!" All we had here was a cart track then. On one part of my round, at Scotvin, I had to go 11½ miles for just three houses. Things became much easier when we had the causeways.

'There were no fixed hours with the post. I was often out till eight at night, and there was no overtime. At Christmas there were two deliveries a day and I had an assistant because there were twenty-five big mailbags of parcels alone. Then we got all sorts of things going in and out, from cakes and chickens to legs of mutton. I even carried gutted rabbits just in their skin with their legs tied together. People in remote areas such as this have always relied a lot on the post.'

Over ten years Archie had three post horses and became very attached to them. 'The first was Jessie, the second Tommy and last Nelly. I was nearly in tears when Nelly went to the knackery. She was a very wise horse. When she waited while I was delivering she'd have a bite of the long grass. Next day, when we passed the same spot, she would nudge me. All the people loved her, especially the children who sometimes had a ride with me.'

Fortunately, Archie never fell off his trusty steed, but one day he slipped while walking down a brac beside his horse. 'A young girl was watching me and she clapped her hands with glee at the sight of me rolling over. I only twisted my ankle but the doctor sent me by plane to Stornoway.'

In 1964 Archie's life changed dramatically when he acquired his first van, a Morris 600 which cost him £250. 'A chap went with me as co-driver and I took the test the following year. I had sometimes used the tractor for big parcels, but the Post Office stopped me doing this because I was not insured for the road.'

But even the van could be defeated by the elements, such as the time just before Christmas 1973, when Archie had to go up to Clachan for an extra collection. 'I took three bags of cards down to Benbecula just as it started to snow. When I came back out from making the delivery the road was blocked with cars stuck in the snow all over the place. I had to get bed and breakfast and stay there, but three of us finished the bottle that night. The odd thing is that next morning there was not a drop of snow on the road.

'Sometimes it was a job to get the round done with all the hospitality. You had to take the people's dram! So I got a cure for it—I took an empty bottle with me and said: "I'll take it at home". After that they weren't so generous!'

73

Archie retired in 1976, aged sixty. 'Unfortunately I had to go through ill health. I felt all right, but I'd had a little heart trouble and wasn't considered safe to drive the new minibus, which also carried three pensioners. I used to help old people a lot, taking their pension books from the letterboxes and returning with the money next day. One old lady was so pleased her son wrote to the Post Office to sing my praises. Unfortunately it had the opposite effect. I got called up by the head postie and told this could not carry on.'

Although he came from a large family, Archie does not have any children and did not marry until he was fifty-one. But his happiness is plain to see. Apart from the company of his charming wife, he has the benefit of that wonderful Western Isles community spirit. And as if that isn't enough, there's a wealth of wildlife, too—anyone would be envious of the otters on his doorstep, even though they do sometimes raid neighbouring crofts to steal the hens.

The Uists, including Grimsay, are very special places steeped in history, of which Archie is well aware. 'We used to get a lot of bones at the end of this island from all the sailors drowned at sea. And there are ancient monuments everywhere. Just after the last war there was a man down there built a croft with stones from the old temple, and he used to say he could hear voices at night.' Whatever that crofter heard, surely it could not have been more fascinating than the life of Archie Macdonald.

FROM THE ARCHIVES

Valuable Sea-weed

THE epicure and the poor sea-side cottager both seemed to have derived profit from the sea-weeds. The former has long enjoyed his famous 'laver sauce', and the 'dulce' of the Highlander is both food and medicine. Even the sheep and cattle that graze on our rocky coasts have learned the value of the sea-weeds, and may be seen wandering among the rocks in search of some approved delicacy.

From W. Furneaux's *The Outdoor World* (1905)

SAILING FOR OYSTERS

FRANK COCK AND
FRANK VINNICOMBE

FISHERMEN OF CORNWALL

Frank Vinnicombe

Frank Cock

Red-breasted merganser

THANKS to an 1868 byelaw prohibiting the use of motors while fishing, Western Europe's last fleet of working sailboats still harvests the oysters of the Carrick Roads, at the mouth of Cornwall's River Fal. Truro City Corporation—since superseded by Carrick County Council—also decreed that the oysters should only be taken from 1 October to 31 March, between 9am and 3pm Monday to Friday, and 9am to 1pm on Saturday. As a result, the Fal fishery continues to thrive while other oyster beds have been wiped out, and we are allowed a glimpse of a way of life which has scarcely changed since Roman times. But it also remains a tough way to earn a living, attracting only the most resilient of characters. Frank Cock and Frank Vinnicombe have been among the most successful this century.

At his secluded home on Restronguet Creek, the still very active Frank Cock, whose father died at ninety-six and mother at ninety, told me about his Cornish upbringing. The youngest of three children and christened George Francis, he was born 'just up the creek' at Point, on 2 December 1905. His grandfather was the skipper of a coastal schooner and his father a gardener/coachman and yachtsman for the Chellew shipping family.

Frank remembers his childhood with great clarity. 'At Devoran school the postman used to bring lunch up for me and my sisters. It was mostly hot pasties. Devoran was a very busy port then, with a tram-line from Redruth serving the tin smelting works at Penpol. Many ships brought in coal and pit props for the mines and took away the tin. Mother could remember seven Norwegian vessels moored out here in the creek, bringing pit props. And I can remember two small coastal steamers—the *Eremus* and *Trefusis*—bringing coal from South Wales.

'They had mud pilots here too, men with other jobs who came down when needed. In winter they put hurricane lamps on poles along the creek to show ships the way in at night. It was about then I saw my first aeroplane, writing '*Daily Mail*' in the sky with smoke signals.

'It was very hot, steamy and smelly in the smelting works, where my uncle was a foreman and the men worked shifts. Wagons pulled by teams of six or eight horses brought the ore from the mines; after each delivery the horses grazed on Point green.

'There were several fishing boats here, but not much commercial. It was mostly nets and you could go out and catch fish any time, they was that plentiful. As kids we used to roll up our trousers and run our hands along the bottom in the shallows. When we found a plaice we used to flip it up onto the dry mud. And there were masses of mackerel and bass in the river here. Nothing like it now. People used to say to Father: "Have you got a bass?", and he'd say: "No, but I'll 'ave one tomorrow", 'e was that sure of it.'

The Cock family certainly never went short of food. 'Father was a bit of a poacher too, and there was lots of rabbits as well as the odd pheasant. During the '14–18 war he had a smallholding and kept a few fowls and a couple of cows which were fattened for the market.

'During the first war Father went to sea in a ketch called the *WJC* which belonged to a cousin, William John Cock. They carried anything, but mostly coal, ammunition, lots of horses and horse meal over to France. I remember once they brought back the dead horses, which were made into bone meal and tanned hides at Penryn.'

Despite having to stay home from Devoran school with 'paralysis' (polio) for twenty months, Frank passed the exam for Truro College, where he went at the age of twelve. But he always wanted to be a fisherman 'or something on the sea', so at the age of fifteen he started helping his father. 'Chellew had died and left Father the boat he used to run. Father converted the *Ida* to oyster fishing.'

At first Frank had no set wage, 'but we only worked from nine to one o'clock on Saturday and the money we had then was my perks. Oysters were then about £2 10s 0d a thousand. But I only had two winters with Father, as things got so bad with the Depression. Father said: "There's no prospects 'ere boy: you better learn a trade."

'I went to old man Hitchings, who was a very good boatbuilder, but he wasn't taking on any more apprentices so I went into Falmouth docks with Cox & Co. I finished my five-year shipwright apprenticeship in 1927 and stayed there till 1929, when things got bad and I was on the dole part of the time. So I went on the buildings house carpentering till the yard was busy again.'

Frank married in 1930 and went to live at Falmouth, above the sweetshop which his wife managed. 'We were there four years and in the process I lost some teeth! We came back to Restronguet when my wife got pregnant and we rented the house next door to here for thirty-five years. My parents lived in this house then.

'When the war came I couldn't get out of the docks as we got very busy. Towards the end of the war the Americans had a repair base at Mylor dockyard and I was made up to chargehand. Because of all the local naval interest the area was bombed a lot. My brother-in-law was killed in a daylight raid on Falmouth docks, and there were lots killed in Mylor, too.

'In 1946 I came out on my own oyster fishing, and in the summer started to run a passenger boat for tourists. I acquired an ex-RAF seaplane tender which took twelve on day trips, mostly to Looe and Polperro. I needed to earn a livin' all year round as I never found any fortune. The best thing I ever dredged up was a big ol' coil of copper wire, which I sold for £45.

'In 1949, in partnership with Harry Barnes, I bought the *Morning Star* off Billy Harris for £250. She was said to be 136 years old then! That first winter we had to bail out sixty buckets of water every drift as she was leakin' so bad. One day it was blowin' a bit fresh, so I said to my mate under the coamings [side decking], where there was a bit of shelter: "What time is it?" And without looking at his watch he said: "It's 10.30". I said: "How do you know that?", and he replied: "I can see the mail van at Mylor Dockyard through the seams in the boat!" It turned out the weight of wind in the sails and everythin' had really opened the boat up, so at the end of that season I set to work on her.'

Remarkably, Frank managed to keep the *Morning Star* afloat and work her right up to 1980 when, very sadly, at over 167 years old, she was sunk by an unidentified boat. 'I woke up one morning and when I looked out over the creek here all I could see was the top of the mast. It was one of the saddest days of my life.

'I got a Flushing diver in to raise her. He put air bags forward and aft to lift her up, but one bag came out and up under the bowsprit, lifted it up and forced the foredeck down into the fore peak. He re-set the bags and the same thing

Morning Star *was built in the early nineteenth century*

happened aft, under the boom. It was one hell of a mess. Anyhow, we got her up in the end and took her down to Terry Heard's boatyard. He said it would cost about £5,000 to put right, so I said "Forget it—you can have her!", as I was thinking about retirement anyway.

'After that she was laid up for several years, Terry died and young Martin Heard took over the yard. One day Peter de Savaray's agent came round lookin' for an old boat and Martin said, "I've just the thing for you". As a result, *Morning Star* ended up in "The Last Labyrinth" museum at Land's End—but only half of her, as they cut her down the middle, lengthways, to fit her in!'

Although Frank and his father used to catch as many as four thousand oysters in one day, Frank has only eaten one in his whole life. 'I don't like the taste.'

Fortunately others have always been more enthusiastic, especially the French. 'We used to lay a lot of oysters on beds along the foreshore, where they were

'*Father was a bit of a poacher*'

exposed at low tide, and the French came over to collect them in one big lot at the end of the season. But the landowners tried to stop us laying them on the foreshore, so all the fishermen got in touch with their MPs and took it to the High Court. Luckily we won the right to continue, and after that every 5 November— the day of our victory—has been taken as a holiday on the River Fal. One of the ways we celebrate is to race for the silver oyster trophy.

'Today the bye-law says the oysters have got to be able to dry out on good spring tides, so that means they are covered most of the time. The beds are marked by sticks.

'Later I sold mostly through the Duchy of Cornwall oyster farm at Port Navis, on the Helford River, but also to a merchant at Flushing—at first by boat, but then by lorry twice a week.

'Another thing my partner and I used to do was deliver yachts, and in 1963 we sailed one over to the River Twistle, near Clacton. The Essex fishery had just lost the majority of their oysters in that record cold winter, so when the merchants there found out what we did, they asked us to send up a couple of hundred sample oysters. Next season they bought everything we caught and they paid us much better money than the Cornish merchants; so I dealt with them for the next twenty years.

Frank Cock proudly poses with Morning Star *in 1976, after the early-nineteenth-century boat had been given a refit*

'I used to go back with the merchant at the end of the season to re-lay our oysters on the Essex beds at West Mersea. Apparently our oysters grew quicker to marketable size up there and you wouldn't have recognised 'em after six months: must have been something in the water.'

Even in later years, when most people would be more interested in sitting on the quayside smoking a pipe, Frank has remained very active. And not surprisingly, most of his interests have revolved around the sea, especially sailing, both racing for fun and helping out in the Restronguet Sailing Club rescue boat. 'My last big trip out was in 1992, when I went over to France with Martin Heard, to a gathering of classic boats.'

Years before that there was one race which gave Frank a few unexpectedly exciting moments, when he was in a regatta at Penryn. 'As we turned very tight on a mark, under the watchful eye of an enthusiastic crowd, we jibed closer to the quay than intended and the boom swept two people into the water. Luckily no one was hurt. Billy Harris was then *Morning Star*'s owner and skipper.

Competitively, Frank has been equally successful ashore. Proudly he recalls that in 1989 he won the pool shield down at the nearby Pandora Inn—which has been licensed since the fourteenth century and fronts Restronguet Creek— exactly fifty years after he won the skittles shield there. Since then he has become very interested in knot-making, some of which work he has framed and auctioned

Outside the old Pandora Inn, Mylor Bridge: Frank Cock (centre) with the skittles shield he had won back in 1939. Pictured right is his partner, Harry Barnes

for charity. He has also taken up wood turning, his creations having a distinctly maritime influence; not the least of these is an impressive lighthouse.

Despite leading such an active life, Frank has managed to avoid disaster at sea. His only bad accident happened ashore, though indirectly it was attributable to the water. 'It was some ten years ago on New Year's Day and I thought it was about time I got down to pump the boat out. Well, it had been snowing a fair bit and on the way I slid down out here, fifty-four feet all the way down through the bushes and over the sloping cliff face. Not surprisingly I was knocked out, and the next thing I remember was waking up in my kitchen with a cup of tea, kindly provided by my rescuer, Ray Frost, also a local fishermen.' As he was then in his mid-seventies, Frank was very lucky not to have come off worse.

Equally tough is Frank Cock's second cousin, Frank Vinnicombe, whose son is the sixth generation of fishermen in his family. I accompanied Frank Vinnicombe one day in January to see how this seventy-year-old managed to put in such a hard day's work on the oyster beds.

'I can remember seein' my Gramfer Frankie tapdancin' on the end 'ere when 'e was almost eighty', Frank told me as we set out in his sailboat *Shadow*. The 1886-built gaff-rig cutter still has its original oak frame. 'The wood was cut down on a local estate— Carclew—and brought down on a big, horse-pulled hay wagon. The whole lot only cost 2/6d, but Hitchings the boatbuilder thought that a bit stiff at the time.'

Christened Frederick Francis, Frank was born on 26 October 1923 at Mylor. 'I started helping Dad at eight years old, pushin'

Frank Cock's father could always be relied upon to catch a bass

Frank Cock dredging for oysters aboard Morning Star

a cart round to sell fish before I went to school. Fishin' was always the big thing, but Dad made me do a 4½-year mason's apprenticeship so that I had a second string in case anythin' went wrong. Later on I was able to build my own house, and I've got a little fish shop alongside it, which I open once a week for locals. My son did an apprenticeship too, as a boatbuilder.

'It's been a very unpredictable life, but I wouldn't swap it for anythin', despite all the changes. Back in Grandad's day oysters fetched as little as 2/6d a thousand, and the Frenchmen used to come over in a big ship in March and April to pay the men with golden sovereigns at the Pandora Inn. I've seen six or seven landlords come and go there. The customers used to be all fishermen, but now it's mostly summer yachties and tourists.'

From the age of eighteen until he was twenty-three Frank was in the RA—the

Frank Vinnicombe manoeuvres Shadow for another drift over the oyster beds. To the left is a cultch board, to the right some of his dredges

(Left) Seagulls are Frank Vinnicombe's constant companions

7–9th Cameronians. 'We were mostly on London defence, but went into France on D-Day. Twice I got shrapnel in my back and legs and couldn't wait to get back. I suppose I was bloody lucky. We left some good boys out there, and if ever there was a wasted time in my life that was it. The first thing that we notice whenever we go out the county is that everyone is rushin' around to die. When we came back from the war I made up me mind to enjoy meself and do what I want to do. Now I've got no need to come out 'ere today, or next week or next month, but I love it.'

Frank was very obviously a man in tune with nature as we motored up Mylor creek towards the oyster beds. Suddenly there was a young gull beside him at the helm. 'Oh, he's come for his biscuits', Frank explained. 'They always come down at the same point. I feed the parents and then each generation knows it's safe to follow, only this one's goin' to be disappointed as I've forgotten the dog biscuits today. We'll find a few crumbs of cake for him later.' But this bird wanted immediate attention and swooped down to seize Frank's hat, which it promptly dropped in the sea. Quite unperturbed, Frank put about and his young assistant, Kevin, scooped the sodden headgear from the water. 'It's no problem', said Frank, 'there's heaps of hats in there'. And without further ado he popped the wet hat beneath the engine cover to dry off.

'You always know when you're going to get a cold night out here because these birds will come down on your cultch board [on which the oysters are separated from all the rubbish] and feed like mad on the crabs and other bits we bring up.'

Frank explained how 99 per cent of the Fal oysters were wiped out by the disease *bonamia* in 1981. 'I lost £9,000 worth of stock in a month and there was no compensation—not a bloody ha'penny. The French had sent me the sacks, labels and so on, and came over at the end of the season, but all the oysters were dead. After that the ministry didn't allow the transfer of oysters up to Essex and they closed us down for three years. Before the disease there were up to thirty boats out here, and in 1925 there were a record fifty sailboats and eighty-seven haultow punts; but in 1984 I was about the only one left.

'There was another big setback in the late seventies when the "Klondykers" polluted the beds.' There were about fifteen of these huge, foreign factory ships, served by a fleet of some thirty 'catcher' vessels, mainly from Scotland, which plundered one of the world's last great mackerel stocks. The Carrick Roads were badly affected by oil, both accidentally and deliberately discharged through cleaning out of tanks. Also, any catcher boat that could not sell its haul would dump the excess overboard and the decomposing fish reduced the water's oxygen content below the critical level at which oysters can exist. Furthermore, the fish bodies fouled the oyster dredges, and the mackerel stock was so depleted that many of the local men lost their summer fishing.

Only oysters which cannot pass through the ring may be kept for sale

In 1982 the Government stepped in, but it was too late. Yet the pressure to allow purse-seine nets back has continued—and if ever such greedy practices were reinstated, the oyster fishery would be jeopardised once more. 'As it is there's no youngsters comin' into it', said Frank. 'It's not so bad for me with my own boats and equipment all paid for, but how can a young chap hope to pay off the bank? I have a second boat—a Cygnus 32 built for handline mackerel fishin'—and we've been hopin' against hope that the mackerel will come back as the demand for oyster's so poor.

'In the autumn the mackerel come up from the west and migrate east, and if you want to catch 'em you've got to go after 'em. In March they migrate west again. I fish from Mount's Bay, Newlyn, to Salcombe in Devon, always for one day only as the fish must be fresh. But it's a long day, sixteen to eighteen hours, and this winter mackerel season [1992–3] has been the worst for years, with howlin' gale after gale. The seas out here have been mountainous, and have driven the fish right off. The longer a settled period there is, the better the fishin'. Although they're in their natural habitat, no fish likes bein' thrown this way and that. It's been so bad they've 'ad the mackerel crews goin' round pickin' daffodils and things. But despite everything this winter we've still been able to stick up at least two or three species of fresh fish in my shop each week. You can't do much better than that.

'All our mackerel are caught on hurdy-gurdies, with fifty to sixty hooks a set, but it's all hydraulic winders now. In winter we use size 16 or 18 hooks and plastic tubes to attract the fish, but much smaller hooks and feathers are good in the spring when the water's clear and the fish are near the surface. It's because it's all hook and line they're such lovely fish. Those caught in purse-seines are limp and soft because they've drowned in the net. They're nothin' like ours to eat.

'I used to catch mackerel on this oyster boat, but she'd only take 150 stone and would then be right down with the weight. We sell to the big markets at Looe and Plymouth. Italy will take all we can get, Greece too: they eat a lot of oily fish out there. At the moment [1993] we only get £1.50 a stone for good small and medium mackerel iced down into two-stone boxes—but they are transported straight to Italy at £6 a stone, so somebody does well out of it! Also, ninety per cent of the white fish and crabs and lobsters are exported to the Continent now.

'In the early seventies there were three hundred handliner boats, with two to four crew per boat, and nine packing co-operatives serving the mackerel down here, so the Scots put a thousand men out of work with their purse-seines. And because the mackerel went, the pressure was put on all the other fish. Everyone 'ad to do somethin' else.

'But at least it's lookin' good now as far as the oyster stock goes. The only trouble is the demand's gone. The Government put all their research into the Pacific oyster, which costs less and is disease-free. Unfortunately most people have so few oysters they can't tell one from another. Ours is the only true native British species – the European flat oyster. If someone could get the marketin' goin' we could support fifteen to twenty sailboats out here. Grandad always said there was a good steady livin' for fifty men. But at the moment [1993] all we get is twenty bloody pence for each fish, that's £20 a hundred in sizes one, two and

The gull swooped down to seize Frank Vinnicombe's hat

three. The merchant gets at least twice that, and then there's the shop or restaurant mark-up. What we need is some young blood in the business, someone with a 1990s outlook. Trouble is the present merchants are old like me and don't have much interest in improvin' things.

'In the late fifties my brother and me had ten thousand oysters in this boat on one day and they fetched £3 a thousand. But when they're so heavy as that you

When he caught this 20lb hake in 1960, Frank Vinnicombe broke a British record which had stood since 1911

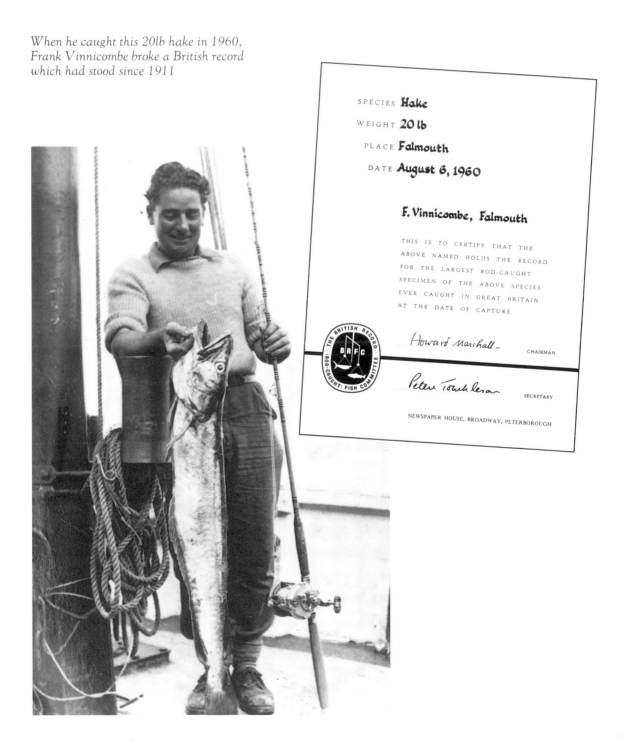

SPECIES **Hake**

WEIGHT **20 lb**

PLACE **Falmouth**

DATE **August 6, 1960**

F. Vinnicombe, Falmouth

THIS IS TO CERTIFY THAT THE ABOVE NAMED HOLDS THE RECORD FOR THE LARGEST ROD-CAUGHT SPECIMEN OF THE ABOVE SPECIES EVER CAUGHT IN GREAT BRITAIN AT THE DATE OF CAPTURE

Howard Marshall CHAIRMAN

Peter Tombleson SECRETARY

NEWSPAPER HOUSE, BROADWAY, PETERBOROUGH

don't get the money, because the fish merchant will make sure he drops the price on 'e. After the disease struck, catches were down to as little as twenty a day.

'I eat a few myself—I like 'em best out the shell and deep-fried in batter, with a squeeze of lemon juice—but I'd rather have a nice bit of fish!'

The oysters are caught in the winter because they breed in the summer. Each shellfish produces about a million eggs, but mortality is very high among the free-swimming larval stage. After about seven to nine days drifting up and down—'that's why you need a long estuary'—when the water temperature reaches about 15°C, the larvae, which are only the size of a pinhead, drop down onto the beds and must find fairly clean rocks or pieces of shell to which they attach themselves. They are then known as 'spat', and spend the next couple of years putting down layers of shell on their way to marketable size.

Frank's two-man boat carries four dredges, and for each a £100 seasonal licence fee is payable to Carrick County Council. Anyone can apply for such a licence and fish anywhere on the Carrick Roads, so with the opening up of the European market local fishermen now fear overseas competition, especially from the French and Spanish. 'But we don't get any subsidies from Europe, and from last week every bag has got to be labelled saying where from, which bank, who it's goin' to, name of boat, operator and so on. All this hassle and you don't get anythin' better for it.'

It is not really surprising that Frank Vinnicombe is so fit and strong, because each dredge is some 3ft wide and weighs about 30lb so that it stays on the seabed. Hauling these up and down for six hours or so is no task for the faint-hearted, especially when being buffeted by gales. 'I've seen boats out 'ere in nor'westers which blew the canvas right out their sticks. Wouldn't happen now, though—this nylon's too strong. But you've got to 'ave wind for these boats, no light airs. Gramfer always used to say: "Sunshine and oysters don't mix". Just that bit more blow and you'll drag the oysters out better.'

The dredgerman must be an expert sailor too, not only with intimate knowledge of the tides and oyster beds, but also able to make a boat drift in the right direction at just the right speed: too slow and the dredge will fill with mud, too fast and it will skip over the oysters. He must also make an infinite number of variations to the sail, to allow for constant changes in conditions, so his anticipation must be first-class and his actions prompt. At the end of each drift, which involves dropping the dredges a number of times, he must be able to sail back to start another with maximum speed. 'Now look here', said Frank, 'we're shakin' out the reefs to increase the sail area, else we'll never get back with this breeze. You've got to 'ave complete control of the boat at all times. It's all right on a day like this, but some days the spray's all over and you're more like a duck. By the way, that's the third mast I've 'ad on *Shadow*: they go soft after a while; and that's the third deck.'

But despite all the skill, the average dredge picks up only some fifteen per cent of oysters. Also, you have to take account of the fact that 'Your oyster dredge is a lot more efficient on a low tide as he bites more.'

After so many years of practice, Frank exudes efficiency, yet rarely appears to hurry. Also, he never appears to look up to find favoured spots—I think he could

fish blindfold and catch more than most people—but he does like a good blow so that the boat can perform well. Nonetheless, there are always days when it is either too calm or too rough to work efficiently and then the beds get a rest—further ensuring survival of the fishery.

'See that mainsail—that's the first terylene one on *Shadow*. I put it up for £30 about fifteen years after the war. The old boys up 'ere didn't like the look of that—they all had cotton, which was red because it was dipped and tanned to stop the rot. But you still 'ad to hoist them up and dry them out once a week to prevent the stitches falling out. Now there's no such thing as rotting—it's all man-made fibres. But it's also got all out of proportion with prices: I've just had to pay £60 for a small jib.

'You need the gaff-rig for fine tuning. You see, you're takin' landmarks all the time to find the best beds. You can't do that with a Bermudian [Bermudan] rig— that's either up or down. With that the mast would have to be 'alf as high again.' As it is, oyster sailboats average 22–30ft long and have tall polemasts and long bowsprits. They're still making boats like these in GRP (Glass Reinforced Plastic), but the wooden ones are steadier to dredge. Bigger boats such as the *Shadow* are open rather than flush-decked to avoid repeated bending in handling the oyster trays, and the draught is usually restricted to some 5ft to facilitate working over the shallows.

Even so, there are many areas where the sailboats cannot work through lack of space or wind, and there the haultow punts come into their own. These 16ft 'winkboats' employ hand winches, because they, too, must comply with the no-engine rule. 'Down here they've always been known as Coombe Kaffirs. But I don't know why', said Frank.

Despite being out in all weathers for so many years, Frank has never been sunk or even gone overboard, 'though I've lost the crew once or twice. I just throw a buoy at 'em and shout "Hold on!" till we come round again.

'We had a hectic time back in '63, during that awful cold. There were fifteen or sixteen yachts sunk out here and I had the job of bringin' a lot of 'em back up because I had a big Scotch boat then, with all the winching gear. We never used to wear gloves then and it was so cold gettin' oysters my crew used to put his hands in the warm diesel. Half the birds were starving, and when the poor redwings tried to get from one side of the harbour to the other they just fell in the water—the blackbacked gulls came down eating 'em like nuts.'

Frank, too, has had some unusual pickings from the sea, but there has been no real treasure. 'I've never found a pearl, but then the proper ones grow in a different species and I don't think the water's really warm enough for 'em down here. In any case we don't open the oyster shells. I've heard there's been one or two green ones.

'But after the war we was snaggin' everything, from a Jeep to dozens of rifles, ammunition and shells. It took a long time to clear that lot up. Since then I've had two or three outboard engines, lots of rods, false teeth and everythin'. See, every summer this is all yachties up 'ere and they drop things overboard. There's not so much really old stuff, but I've had a few cannonballs and pre-war lemonade bottles with the marble stoppers. We also used to catch quite a lot of rays and skate in the dredges, but not so many now. Occasionally we get a few big stones, but there aren't many of those left because we always dump 'em ashore.'

Despite such heavy work, some of the dredges which Frank uses have lasted for many years. 'I had some of these made just after the war, but those up 'ome were made by Grandad.'

When a dredge is hauled up it is first shaken near the surface to expel all the mud, and then emptied into a tray and the 'cultch' of oysters, shells, crabs and stones quickly sorted. Using a culling knife called a 'cultack', a roughly-shaped

A modest day's haul of saleable oysters for Frank Vinnicombe

To make the most of limited dredging time, Fal oyster fishermen must be first-class sailors

Skipper Frank Vinnicombe (centre) and delighted clients after a successful day's sharking aboard Shadow

piece of flattened iron, Frank cleans off and sorts the oysters, the 'freshcaught' for immediate sale going into one bucket, 'bed' oysters for 'growing on' into another. But none may be removed if they pass through the 2⅝in brass ring provided by the licensing authority. In practice, Frank rarely needs this because his eye is so experienced. 'Now that's what we're looking for—a nice fat fish', he declares. 'You can go by the weight in your hand more than anythin'.'

Even when you are well positioned you cannot simply throw the dredges overboard and hope for the best. There must be constant attention to matters such as the length of the rope: 'Shorten up Kev—the seabed's jumped right up at us!'

Any crabs brought up are immediately pounced on by the ever-present gulls. 'It's nice to see birds like that: you've never got much mess left on the boat when they've been round.' Predators such as the oyster drill may be killed, but harmless creatures such as sponges are tipped back overboard along with the essential cultch to provide anchorage for spat. With such a caring attitude, rarely has it been necessary for shells to be brought in from another fishery.

While larger oysters provide a modest immediate income—just 215 were taken by Frank and his assistant on the day of my visit—the bed oysters command a higher price after the season has closed. 'They're like a little nest egg—just like a crop of plants on the ground.' However, they also attract a higher mortality rate as they are susceptible to cold weather along the tideline. Furthermore, about a third of the brood oysters sold to merchants for fattening die in the summer as they are so weakened through spawning or 'dredge knock'—damage caused during capture.

Before being consumed, the oysters are put into purification tanks where they are kept under ultra-violet light for thirty-six hours to kill all bacteria present.

When times were better, Frank used to have tanks ashore and employed two men to look after them so that he could cut out the middle man, 'but disease put paid to that. You can't be out here and up there. I used to supply the Savoy Restaurant and Savoy Grill, Scott's Eating House and Simpson's in the Strand.

'I used to take two ton of oysters three times a week to Whitstable, but that was all lost in '63, when the ice on the sea took up all the oysters they laid. The Whitstable fishery went bust and they didn't get a ha'penny compensation, even though they had all my receipts.

'But this is a lovely job. You've only got yourself to please—no phones or anythin'. Within reason you can sit down when you want, but there's plenty of

Killer whale

exercise and you never get really cold because workin' the ropes keeps the circulation goin'. What you get is what you catch, so you can't blame anyone else.'

The subject of fitness has been particularly important to Frank because up to 1990 he was a highly successful boxing coach. 'I'm the only advanced coach Cornwall's ever had and I've often been up to help the national coach. I'm proud to say I've brought on half a dozen internationals, and at one time in our local club we had seven open-class boxers.

'Dad was a referee and I boxed before the war, when it was all betting. In those days they said I was only interested in the three Bs—boxing, booze and boats. Now I don't drink either, so there's just the boats!'

But there was at least one occasion when Frank's boxing experience proved useful on board. For many years he has taken out anglers, most of whom are well behaved and remain calm even in a crisis. 'But one day in the fifties I was out sharkin' with this proper panic bloke. The weather was beautiful, but suddenly up came this violent storm and you could hear the hailstones hittin' the sea. We had the missen up and we started to spin round like anythin'. Well, this chap got more and more agitated, saying this was just like a typhoon he'd seen in India. Eventually he panicked so much I 'ad to punch him and lay him out. But in ten minutes it was all over, the sun was out, the deck steaming and I was trying to sort out lines, sharks, blood and shit and everythin'. The thing is, the storm brought the sharks on to feed like anythin' and we had six or seven on at once.'

Fortunately, most people are a pleasure to take out and some have taken regular fishing holidays with Frank for over thirty years. 'The only bad thing about taking groups out for so long is that they all go in the end. I say to one: "Where's old Jack this time?", and they always seem to reply: "Oh, he died last year".

'Then there was one occasion when I waited and waited and the party never turned up. It wasn't like them not to let me know, but I heard later that on the way down they'd driven into a lamp-post and some of them were killed outright. People come down here from the Black Country, Kent and all over the place, so they're always in a rush.'

Frank is also a very accomplished angler himself, and has held the rod records for no less than six British species—hake (20lb), whiting (8lb), and blue, mako, porbeagle and thresher sharks. 'I had the first two sharks caught in this area, on a rod from this boat. The local shark club started just one year after the one at Looe. In 1955 I took the local tackle shop man out and the first day we had two blues of 105lb and 95lb. Altogether there's been over ten thousand sharks caught from my boats.

'Back in the fifties, sixties and seventies we used to catch fifteen to twenty sharks a day over about two months each year. It was a very popular sport then and at one time I had three shark boats goin'. Everythin' was boomin' then in the West Country. There were no jets takin' everybody off to Spain, and all the guest houses was full of young people and factory workers from all over. As soon as they introduced the big jets that finished it.'

Frank also had some very distinguished regulars among his shark catchers. 'It was quite the thing to come down 'ere sharkin' in the fifties and sixties. Jack Hawkins, the film star, used to bring his family down—he was a nice chap. I named one of my boats after the *Compass Rose* in his film 'The Cruel Sea'. Other celebrities who came included Teezy Weezy the hairdresser, actress Belinda Lee, Lenny Peters of Peters and Lee, and Winston Churchill—the present MP. We even had the Russian ambassador out, and when he came the KGB men took the floorboards up lookin' for bombs.'

Today Frank still accommodates parties of anglers, and knows many good marks some fifty to sixty miles off. 'We work a sunken convoy of wrecks—the U-boats had 'em.'

With such a fine reputation, Frank has no difficulty in finding customers for his charter boat, which is as well because some of the locals can cause problems. 'Falmouth has grown out of all proportion in recent years and is not what it was. Sometimes when the drunks pile out of the night clubs they take our sharking signs by the boats, and those advertisin' boards are quite expensive.'

Over so many years afloat, Frank has seen many accidents and helped to rescue numerous people. 'There's a lot of yachtsmen go overboard. When they get out 'ere a lot of 'em go stupid as though it's their last day, and then they come unstuck.

'I suppose the worst incident I can remember was when the *Darwin* sank in the seventies and thirty-two people drowned. I was out sharkin' that day and it was bad enough in my big ship, but all these people had was a pleasure cruiser that was open aft. You've got to know your coast. No witnesses survived so nobody knew what really happened. They simply set out for the day from that big grey building over there and never returned. Whole families was wiped out. It wasn't till next day that we knew they was missin'—when we heard these Shackletons buzzin' up and down. About a week to ten days later the bodies started comin' up and when I found one I radioed the coastguard. Very sad. There was all their 'andsome cars—Rovers an' all—parked over there at the hotel for weeks after. Greatwood House is now luxury flats.'

There have been air crashes, too. 'One Sunday four years ago a chap came down here with a Sopwith Super Marine replica and there was a very strong easterly wind when the plane started to spit and sputter and bits of the tailplane dropped off. He came down on the shore over there and was killed outright. Very sad to see. We were having a re-fit in Mylor dockyard at the time. I've never been up in a plane in me life.

'I've seen training helicopters from Cauldrose ditch out here as well. One we had right close to us when we were mackerel fishin'. The two chaps got out of it all right and we offered to tow them, but they said no. They had to wait for the Navy support vessel to come up. But they went at it like a bull at a gate and towed 'em in too fast, so they sunk. What they should have done was let us tow them in gently with two lines attached.'

But accidents happen on fishing boats, too. Frank told me about 'a Mevagissey man who had a shark on a gaff and it came off and bit his arm. Funny thing was it weighed 70lb and he had seventy stitches, so it was like the fish gettin' its own back. Luckily I've still got all my fingers, but there's some skippers round here with a few missin'. Sometimes they get a wire trace round a finger and lose it when the shark suddenly pulls away.'

Fishermen must also remain vigilant in case of serious pollution incidents. Frank's most anxious time was when the *Torrey Canyon* went aground on the Seven Stones Reef in 1967 and discharged 120,000 tonnes of oil off Land's End. 'I was down with two boats helpin' with the spraying and had to wear masks, gloves and goggles. We were very lucky because one more night and we would have had all the oil up 'ere and we couldn't rely on the booms across the harbour. Fortunately the wind changed into the north for a week and took most of it over to France.'

But while Frank cares deeply for the environment and is on the side of wildlife generally, like many of the best conservationists he also firmly believes in culling fur, fin and feather for pest control or food when the harvest is sustainable. He still has two gundogs and believes that 'fishin' and shootin' go hand in hand'. Like many fishermen, he has often had a dog on board and has shot quite a lot of wildfowl. 'But I'm not keen on ducks now. What I really like is roughshootin' ashore for a few woodcock, and we get a lot of those down this way.

'I used to keep a pack of ten pair of beagles for foxes—the Mylor Hounds. The Roseland pack took mine when I finished. You've got to be fit for that job. It all fits in well with nature—huntin', shootin' and fishin'.'

As we spoke, I noticed a few redbreasted mergansers near the shore. 'They come down every winter', said Frank, 'and go back in March. Regular as clockwork these birds, and you can always rely on them. Watch the birds and you won't go far wrong. Watchin' nature—that's what this job's all about.

'When it's goin' to blow up a bit the crows always go back early across the creek to their roost. If there's rain on the way the gulls always dip themselves in the water, and if they take an object up in the air and drop it, then watch out because there's a storm brewin'. And out mackerelin' I always watch the gannets for signs of activity: they're the greatest fishermen.'

Cornish fishermen also have plenty of sea mammals for company. 'There's hundreds of whales off 'ere, especially the ones with the shark's fin on top—killer whales, and pilot whales, dolphins and porpoises, but we're not too keen on havin' 'em around as they take the mackerel, disperse the shoals and make 'em go down deep. There's plenty of seals, too. They take advantage of the long lines and generally leave just the heads of the fish on the baited hooks. There's one seal out here known as Sammy. He's only got one eye and comes round the boats for fish. Once he tried to grab a conger eel whose tail was hanging over the side of another boat, but the fish got stuck in the scuppers.'

It's not only wildlife which influences Cornish superstition. 'If we're goin' mackerelin' we won't change the tackle on a Friday. And in some places, such as Mevagissey, the fishermen won't set out on a Sunday despite the tides. If necessary they'll wait till one minute after midnight.'

But as we turned about and headed for Mylor, it was a thoroughly confident and contented Frank Vinnicombe who reflected on a life well spent. The flap, flap of the sail was as music to his ears as white, cosy cottages glinted in the weak winter sun on the low hills all around us.

'I thought with all this mild weather we've been havin', and all the primroses up already, the weed would have come on strong, but there's none here yet. You can always tell how advanced the season is by it. As the sunshine increases and the weed grows on the bottom we can't dredge, and I have seen the red collie weed out here as early as January.'

'Don't you ever get tired of this hard slog and having to worry about so many things?', I asked Frank. 'Never', he replied. 'While there's fish to catch and I can get there, I'll be out. I've still got the huntin' instinct in me. But you must keep mixin' with young people to keep you fresh. I say to 'e, look at that: there's people out here in yachts paid thousands of pounds for 'em—and we're doin' the same thing free!'

Hopefully, the *Shadow* will continue to serve Frank well till the day he drops. 'A boat's like a person, really—stop 'em workin' and they've 'ad it! Once the salt's there they're all right, but once you've laid 'em up on the beach they're finished. And if a boat looks lovely at the end of the season then she 'asn't caught no fish. But if she comes in all cut up you know she's done her job. It's only right for a workin' boat to look pretty at the start of the season.'

Unfortunately you cannot touch up and repair the human body so easily as you would a boat. But at least these oystermen of the Fal seem to have weathered well over the seasons. And as a bonus, both my Frank friends have longevity in their blood; indeed, Frank Vinnicombe's older brother still fishes and his mother is fast approaching her one hundredth birthday. No wonder Frank seemed so optimistic when he left me with the words: 'Happy we meet, happy we part, and happy we meet again.'

Sammy, the one-eyed seal

FROM THE ARCHIVES

Capacious Harbour

WE meet with a bay, with a number of creeks, into which the little river Vole discharges itself, on which flood the ancient city Voluba, but it has long since fallen to decay, or lost its name, which remains however in some degree in the sea-port town of Volemouth, or Falemouth. The harbour here is as fine and capacious as that of Brundusium in Italy; one hundred ships may anchor in its several creeks, at such a distance from each other that the tops of the masts of one cannot be seen from another; and it is sheltered from the winds every way by high rocks.

From William Camden's *Britannia* (1586, revised 1789)

BY COMPASS, GUESS AND BY GOD

TOMMY KNOTT

MERCHANT SAILOR AND LIFEBOATMAN OF KENT AND SUFFOLK

Time for a reviver: Tommy brews up on board the Lowestoft lifeboat

DESPITE the fact that both his father and grandfather were farm labourers, Tommy Knott 'only ever wanted to go to sea'. But then he was born beside the briny, at St Margaret's Bay, near Dover. Over three-quarters of a century later, after crossing many a stormy horizon, his outlook is unchanged. In his 'crow's nest' flat above the Royal Norfolk and Suffolk Yacht Club he has a commanding view of Lowestoft Harbour, and is ideally placed to reflect on an often tough and hazardous life. On eventful passage he has helped save many lives and netted two medals for bravery.

Rather appropriately for one destined to spend most of life conquering the sea, he was christened Thomas Victor Knott, but really his second name was inspired by triumph over Germany, for he was born on 13 September 1918. The youngest of three children, he went to the local Church of England school, where he suffered from the then unrecognised condition of dyslexia and 'learnt only two things—religion and gardening'. As a result, he had the greenest of fingers, winning a cup two years running; but the seeds of his nautical career were already sown and he would never follow the furrow ploughed by his ancestors.

'There was no tap or toilet in our house and Father's wage was only £1 12s 6d, but we had an allotment and I think we fed better then than ever since.

'When I was nine I used to help out in a fishing boat which took trippers out round the Goodwin Sands. Then I went in the Sea Scouts and had my first real adventure. At Whitsuntide we bought an old 27ft Montagu whaler for £5—the Navy did us proud, but we still decided to save the cost of transport and sail her ourselves from Chatham to St Margaret's Bay.'

After spending Friday night at Chatham, the seven Scouts went down to the pier at 4am so that they could get underway by 6am, to gain the benefit of the ebb tide down the river. But there was a thick fog and not a breath of wind, so it was not clear enough to set off until 7.45am. They rowed down the Medway, but the fog was still thick in places and navigation was difficult. The *Dover Express* of the day described what happened next:

Off Queensborough the wind freshened from the south-west and the weather cleared slightly. Sail was made, and with a fresh breeze the boat proceeded to pass Garrison Point, along the north coast of the Isle of Sheppey, keeping about 1½ miles off shore.

About noon the sky became very black to the westward, and rain fell. When abreast of the Spaniard Buoy, and about 2½ miles from shore, the wind suddenly veered to the west in a furious squall with heavy, driving rain. Sail had to be shortened at once, and an attempt was made to lower the mainsail. When halfway down something aloft fouled the traveller, and for some seconds things looked nasty, there being a hollow breaking sea and the boat shipping a lot of water. She was, however, brought head to wind, the traveller cleared, and the mainsail stowed.

Owing to the thick rain, all traces of land were lost, so a south-easterly course was set, and shortly afterwards the Columbine Buoy was seen on the starboard bow, and the weather cleared slightly. A number of boats were seen at anchor, which were assumed to be the Whitstable oyster fleet. This enabled an approximate course to be set for Herne Bay, the pier of which was seen about 1 o'clock. The whole of the water to the east coast of the Isle of Sheppey is studded with shoals, some with not more than 1ft of water at low tide, and as it was then low water there was considerable risk of grounding owing to the poor visibility. However, having sighted Herne Bay pier, an easterly course was steered along the coast, and the pier passed at 1.30. The wind was blowing a gale, there was a high following sea, and the boat running before it under a foresail and mizzen, yawed violently and made steering an anxious and tiring task. Continual baling was necessary as the boat shipped a lot of water and the crew were soaked to their skins.

The Reculvers were passed at 2.15, and the tide then being against the wind, made the sea more hollow and dangerous. Margate Pier was passed about 4 o'clock, and soon after the Margate lifeboat, which shortly before had been seen towing a small boat into harbour, was observed to be following the Sea Scouts' boat. It is thought that the lifeboatmen were under the impression that the Scouts were a shipwrecked crew making for shelter, and this is not to be wondered at. Some of the Scouts were in oilskins with uniform caps, some in overcoats, two were wearing scarves round their heads, and the whole boat must have presented a weather-beaten appearance. As the lifeboat came alongside she was hailed and told that the Scouts were bound for Dover, and, after a cheer from her crew, she returned to shore.

The tide was now in full flood, and although the wind continued strong, very little headway was being made. It was hoped that when Foreness was rounded there would be less sea and the wind would be abeam, but, unfortunately, the wind shifted to the south, dead ahead, and the sea was as rough, though not so hollow and breaking as before.

After two beats out to sea and back again, it was found that ground was being

The wind suddenly veered to the west in a furious squall with heavy driving rain. Sail had to be shortened at once, and an attempt was made to lower the mainsail

lost, and being then abreast of the North Foreland, a council of war was held as to whether to run back to Margate, make for Broadstairs or Ramsgate under oars, or beach the boat at Kingsgate and wait until the ebb tide made and then carry on. The crew were tired out, wet and cold, although not by any means depressed, and it was agreed that the best thing would be to put into Broadstairs for the night. The harbour was made about 7.45pm, the boat beached, and the gear left in charge of a fisherman. The party proceeded home by train, arriving at St Margaret's about midnight.

A start from St Margaret's was made at 8 o'clock on Sunday morning and the voyage recommenced at 10.45. In much better conditions the party reached St Margaret's Bay soon after 5pm, having covered over sixty miles. There were three Scoutmasters in the party, but none of them had much experience of such a boat, so, taking everything together, the four lads had had a remarkable first voyage. And for little Tommy Knott that early incident involving a lifeboat was only the first of many—except that in the future he would be the one coming to the rescue.

At first, Master Knott found it very difficult to get a job 'as so many ships were laid up with the Depression. So I became a paper boy for a year. This was a full-time job then, and because I had it I was allowed to leave school at only thirteen and a half years old. My round was six miles twice a day and my pay eight shillings a week.

'I had to save up the £2 10s or so to go to Gravesend Sea School, to train as a deckhand. I needed the money to pay five bob for a medical—of the "cough and you're in" variety—as well as my kit, including oilskin, sea boots and stocking cap. Father couldn't afford it: he didn't want me to go to sea, anyway.

'Discipline was discipline in those days. There were only forty-two lads at the school, but eight instructors. About ten of us were on the *Trident* under Captain Angel and it was a very hard life. One day a lad only chuckled when it was time for lights out and because nobody owned up we all had to stand on deck in our pyjamas, while it was snowing, from 9pm till the mate said "turn to" at 6am!'

Tommy passed out at Gravesend in March 1935 and within a week, at the tender age of sixteen, was aboard his first ship, the *Otira*, bound for Australia and New Zealand. 'There was a crew of about fifty to sixty, with twenty of us crammed together in the fo'c's'le, and there was no heating, so it was very cold going round the Horn and like a furnace crossing the Equator.

'Before we left we loaded up at the Welsh ports—Barry, Cardiff and so on—with two thousand ton of coal in the bunkers and three thousand ton in No 3 hatch—one of the cargo holds, and all the way to Australia us deckhands was takin' that coal out the hatch and topping up the bunkers. It took six weeks to get there, and we burnt ninety ton of coal a day. Our cargo was all sorts of manufactured goods—lots of railway lines, pieces of motor cars and suchlike. In those days Britain supplied the world.

'In Australia we took on wool, tallow, sheep, pigs—all refrigerated. We had twenty-six thousand sheep alone. They'd kill that number in one day out there. At Melbourne there were nineteen ships loading grain for the UK and Europe, and they were nearly all owned by Ericson, the last big owner of the commercial square-riggers. The average age of his crew was only seventeen and he managed

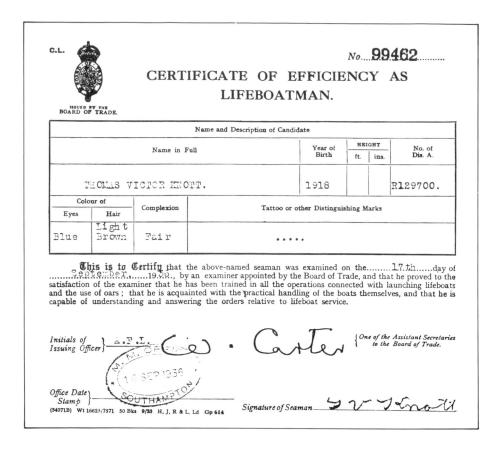

Tommy had only just celebrated his 18th birthday when he qualified as a lifeboatman

to make a profit on grain at only thirty shillings a ton. It was all loaded by carts, each with fourteen horses. My brother was on one.'

For that first voyage Tommy earned £2 5s 0d a month, so when he was paid off on 18 August 1935, after four months and ten days, his gross pay was £10 12s 0d. But by the time his deductions were taken off he was left with only £2 15s 8½d. In those days an able seaman earned £8 5s 0d a month and the minimum hours were eighty-four a week plus two extra on the day of sailing.

For Tommy there followed a long series of voyages as deck boy, ordinary seaman and able seaman, going all over the world for the Royal Mail, Union Castle, Cunard and other lines. He was at the 1935 Spithead Review to witness the apogee of British maritime prestige. And soon after he was on a ship chartered by the Archbishop of Canterbury to take relief supplies to the rebels in Valencia during the Spanish Civil War. He was particularly keen to go when he learned that double time was payable within the three-mile limit, but a brush with Franco's airforce and the commandeering of the cargo plus most of the ship's coal brought sudden revision of his Socialist views. With the Arab stokers deserted, Tommy and his remaining crew mates were more than happy to shovel coal to escape.

When war with Germany was declared, Tommy was in New York unloading

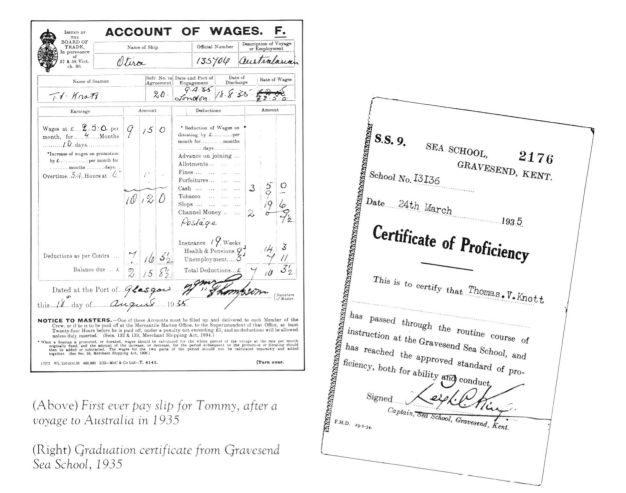

(Above) *First ever pay slip for Tommy, after a voyage to Australia in 1935*

(Right) *Graduation certificate from Gravesend Sea School, 1935*

gold bars from the Cunarder *Aquitania*. 'Chamberlain's message was relayed over the ship's tannoy. Ironically, next day we followed the German liner *Bremen* down the Hudson River.

'When we got home I reported to the nearest Customs office, at Southampton, but was told to go to Chatham, where I ended up with thousands of other Royal Navy Reservists. I was in the RNR till the general service ratings section was disbanded in 1957, and on active service from 1939 to '45.'

At first Tommy was on oilers with the Dover Patrol, and in late 1939 saw dead Germans from a U-boat on the Goodwin Sands. 'Some of them still had their escape apparatus on, and died because they'd vomited into them.'

Later he was aboard an armed merchant ship, with the unexpected luxury of bathroom suites for ratings. Unfortunately, after gun trials there was not one unbroken ceramic aboard. A German torpedo completed the vessel's destruction. Shipless, Tommy was sent to Lowestoft to help arm local boats. There he met Joan, and they married in 1942.

'Being a married man, I didn't want to go back to sea on long voyages after the war, so I answered an advert for a wire splicer at Bentley Colliery, South Yorkshire. It sounded good, with a house and all, but as soon as I got to Doncaster

I realised they just wanted men down the pit. So after six months we went back to St Margaret's Bay and opened a guesthouse with my sister.

'I started doing some painting for the builder who was doing up our house, and before long he went back to London and left me in charge of twelve men renovating five houses for Noel Coward. One of the things I had to do was make three canvas-covered frames for Coward. Each weekend he would paint pictures on them and every week I would have to "white out" his work for another go. But all this soon came to an end because I had no experience of building projects, and after a series of cash crises I left.'

Tommy then had a short spell on coasters, which familiarised him with the restrictive practices of London 'dockies'. 'If the hatches were removed before berthing the dockers refused to offload, but if they were left on they refused to work until they were taken off!

'In 1952 I was the mate of a coaster in Paris when I had a telegram telling me to come home because my father-in-law had died. Then we took over his Woodbine Café in Lowestoft, but it was not profitable—and he had left debts! But eventually we turned it round, bought it, my wife did all the work, and I went in the building trade.

'Then I agreed to take a Wroxham-built boat to the Mediterranean, provided that my £3-a-week wage was paid direct to Joan, to support herself and our son. Unfortunately, the crew supplied by the owner appeared hopeless: two wore glasses and the third had never been on a ship in his life. My fears were well founded. We made several unsuccessful attempts to cross the Bay of Biscay, and the yacht's draught meant that an alternative route via the French canals had to be abandoned at Paris. But other sea jobs followed.

'We still had cash-flow problems, so when my wife saw an advert in the paper for a mechanic on the Lowestoft lifeboat I soon made out an application. But the pay was abysmal and I had second thoughts, so I never posted the letter. But Joan did. I didn't know anything about diesels then, but two ex-seamen came round to interview me and we got on well with a bottle of Scotch.

'Shortly after I was in the Woodbine one night when there was all this bloody banging. It was a policeman at the door and he took me down to the lifeboat. They couldn't get the engine goin' and a ship was in trouble twenty miles away. The radio was on and this bloke was screamin' maydays. This lifeboat chap insisted the petrol was on but I persuaded him to check. As I suspected, it wasn't, so after that they all thought I was hell of a bloke and the job was soon confirmed. I was a stranger to the crew, who were all longshoremen and fishermen, so it was lucky I was able to get on the right side of them before starting the job.'

After twelve years solely as mechanic, 'which worked in well with the Woodbine as I was only three minutes away by bike', Tommy became the first paid coxswain/mechanic. The change in position came about after a most distressing and controversial incident. 'But in any event the old cox was going blind and we'd had two or three incidents where he'd hit a yacht just outside the harbour. It would never happen now. In those days some lifeboatmen were even colour blind, which can be fatal at sea.'

Lowestoft Journal
and Mercury

No. 4973   FRIDAY, DECEMBER 20, 1968   SIXPENCE

LIFEBOAT UNDER NEW COMMAND: FOUR RESIGN

Sequel to criticism of 'no rescue attempt'

LOWESTOFT lifeboat went out last night on a trial of a crew under the command of a new coxswain and second coxswain after a row in which four of the lifeboatmen resigned. The storm among the crew flared into the open this week after criticisms of the part the lifeboat played in Sunday's tragedy on the North Beach when a man died in the sea at the end of a groyne.

Mr. Tom Knott, 50, who on Sunday offered his resign... as a protest...

Below: An airman is winched down from an RAF rescue helicopter in an attempt to save a fisherman in trouble at Lowestoft. Rescuing civilians accounts for more than 90 per cent. of RAF and Navy helicopter missions

Battling in the icy water to free Mr Norman Morrison from the groyne during Sunday's rescue attempts, with Lowestoft lifeboat standing by.

Destined to die: trapped by his foot and pounded by the incoming tide, fisherman Norman Morrison had but a short time to live. Not even the RAF winch man could save him
(Photo: Lowestoft Journal)

On 15 December 1968 brothers Alan and Norman Morrison were fishing in a small boat off Lowestoft when their engine failed. Coastguards saw them baling out and waving their arms so they fired maroons and the lifeboat was slipped and on its way within four minutes. Meanwhile the boat drifted in towards the North Beach and capsized, allowing Alan Morrison to scramble ashore with the aid of police and onlookers. But his brother was suddenly swept against the groyne and his foot became jammed between the steel and wooden piles.

For the next two hours the police, firemen, coastguards and an RAF rescue helicopter fought valiantly against the rising tide and increasingly rough and icy water to free the man, while a horrified crowd watched from the beach just fifty yards away. Every few seconds huge waves broke over Norman Morrison, hiding him beneath a mass of white foam, but time after time he managed to haul himself upright to hang on to the steel pile against which he was pinioned.

A lifebelt was passed to Norman Morrison, who remained surprisingly calm throughout the ordeal. Then a rope was thrown and the trapped man put it round his shoulders. But even with this the foot would not come free. Morrison was urged to pull his foot from the boot, but it was so firmly wedged this was impossible. And all the while the sea was so cold rescuers could not feel their hands and repeatedly had to be hauled back.

When the helicopter arrived, Sergeant Geoff Longmuir—serving his first day with the air-rescue team at RAF Coltishall—was winched down, and battled to free Morrison. The wind battered him against the steel piles, but still he fought to get a line around the man. Exhausted, and with his rubber suit in shreds, the sergeant was winched back up and Flt Lt Cross took over. But his efforts, too, were in vain, and then suddenly their battle was over as Morrison failed to reappear from beneath one massive wave.

It was four days later before the weather was calm enough for police to confirm that the body was no longer there. It had been wrenched free by the violence of the waves, the sea achieving what man and all his sophisticated equipment had failed to do. (Further details of this are contained in the chapter on Fred Morris.)

While rescue attempts were underway the lifeboat had stood close by, but fifty-eight-year-old Harry Burgess, who had been cox for twenty-one years, decided that they could not move right in to help for fear of crushing the man. Not surprisingly, with emotions running high, some of the crew thought otherwise and subsequently Tommy Knott resigned in protest. At this, Burgess and second cox Bill Thorpe also resigned. At the time, Thorpe had commented: 'It is absolutely ridiculous. We did all that we could and stood with tears in our eyes as that man died. We would have done anything, but if the men on the groyne, a fixed platform within a few feet of him, could not help, what could we have done?'

After investigation by the RNLI, no blame was apportioned, but Burgess and Thorpe would not withdraw their resignations and it was Tommy Knott who was invited to become coxswain/mechanic and form a crew urgently. The appointment would prove of great benefit to the local community and visiting sea-goers.

Tommy's first RNLI bronze medal was earned on the morning of 13 April 1974, when red flares were sighted and he took the reserve lifeboat—*Canadian Pacific*—to the assistance of the 41ft Bermudan-rigged yacht *Sarina*. 'Our boat was a 46ft Watson built in 1938, and she was a swine to manoeuvre.

'At 0548 we sighted the *Sarina* five cables east of Benacre Ness. She was lying head to tide, at anchor, and touching bottom in breaking seas. Sails had been furled, but the main was causing considerable windage where it had blown away from the ties. As we attempted to go alongside I noticed that the port engine was only operating at 500rpm and assumed that the propeller had fouled in the shallow water. But I couldn't go down to sort out the problem because I was the cox at the wheel as well as mechanic. It was decidedly worrying. The wind was now north-east, force six to seven, with thirteen-foot breaking waves caused by wind against tide.

'In order to get alongside we went westward of the yacht and, turning to port, a downwind approach was made, during which the lifeboat grounded twice. The yacht's crew were too exhausted to take a line. I decided the only way to get one of us aboard was to put the bow on to her, keeping my screws in deeper water. I stationed second cox Peter Gibbons at the bow and instructed him to board *Sarina* as soon as possible. But as I closed a large sea lifted us and the yacht heeled right over, so I thought I'd struck her bow. I put both engines full astern and as we drew clear Peter jumped across the six feet separating the two boats.

'Peter tried to cut the anchor chain with a hacksaw, but the blade broke. I closed again, threw him the axe, and this time he managed to part the links. Peter then secured a tow-line from the lifeboat's bow to the yacht's rudder head, her auxiliary engine being broken down. But the tow-rope bust, and now there was nothing to stop them going ashore: I thought we'd drown 'em instead of save 'em.

'But I went in again, Peter secured the rope, which we took up at a snail's pace, and made for deeper water. The lifeboat cockpit was continually filling with water and, as the yacht's cabin hatch could not be closed, the speed of tow had to be kept very low. It took us about half-an-hour to do two hundred yards and clear the surf. But then it was easy.

Recognition of outstanding service: Tommy receives an RNLI bronze medal

The cow could only be driven ashore

'We arrived at Lowestoft Harbour at 0723, and it was only then that we discovered there was a fourth crew member aboard the yacht—he'd been out cold down below all the time the others were in the open cockpit! It didn't take me five minutes to put the engine fault right. But even with full power the Watson was all wrong—its shape was like a sailing boat. Peter Gibbons also got the bronze medal for gallantry. He did really well and at one point I'd thought he was a gonner, too.' These were the first medals to be awarded to Lowestoft lifeboatmen since 1943.

Tommy's second bronze medal was earned on 16 August, 1978, when he and his son, Michael, took the pilot cutter *Vivid* to rescue a tug crew. There was only a slight sea when Barkis was out in Lowestoft Roads assisting the 2,625-ton cargo vessel *Jupiter*. But when they tried to put a line aboard to help with steering into harbour ('the ship only had a single screw then, whereas now they have bow thrusters'), what Tommy calls 'the tug phenomenon' happened and the smaller vessel turned right over.

Michael Knott, who was the cox of *Vivid*, heard about the capsize over the radio at about 8.30am and set out immediately after collecting his father from the lifeboat station. Tommy recalls: 'We decided to take the pilot boat because she could do sixteen knots, and we covered the mile or so in three or four minutes.'

Three of the tug's four-man crew were soon rescued, but the fourth could not be seen. Then Tommy spotted a man in the water and dived in fully clothed. 'I just saw his head, but I couldn't really see how he was. I got a line round him but the rope slipped twice, pushing me under water. The pilot boat was high-sided and I was becoming increasingly exhausted with attempts to lift the body, especially as I had just pulled Dieter [one of the crew] aboard. He was covered in oil, and I felt terrible that I couldn't secure a bowline around him before Michael had to pull me aboard. One crew member had clung to a small piece of wood till we rescued him, and skipper Barry Winney had managed to scramble aboard the bow of his upturned boat.' The three rescued had been together in the water for about twenty minutes, trying to keep the lost man afloat.

After helping his father on board, Michael went in search of the missing man, not returning to harbour until 6pm. An RAF helicopter, the Lowestoft lifeboat and other craft were also unsuccessful; the body was washed ashore two days later. While Tommy was awarded a bar to his bronze medal for 'selfless action in entering the water without regard for his own safety', Michael Knott received a framed letter of thanks from the RNLI, in acknowledgement of his 'most praiseworthy speedy action'.

But there have been lighter moments in Tommy's long career. 'One Sunday we were in the club waiting for the bar to open at midday when the coastguard came down and said, would we launch to a cow? The police had just rung to say a cow was in the harbour and the fire brigade plus harbour authorities couldn't get it out.

'So up we went and there was this cow swimming. We got a rope round its neck, but the vet radioed to say don't pull it as it was in calf and would drown. So I decided to drive the cow and run the boat onto the beach—we only drew about 3½ft forward—and the cow could run ashore. This went according to plan, and the poor old thing staggered up the beach exhausted and just stood there.

'We were now aground, and I thought "My inspector's not going to be pleased with us off service for twelve hours till the next tide", so I put my engines full astern. Meanwhile, down through the gate came the police super and the fire chief—both easy to recognise with all that braid—and stood within ten yards of the cow. Suddenly the animal shook itself and charged at them. They moved so fast one of their hats came off, and my crew were laughing fit to burst. But then I realised we'd come straight off the beach and were going full astern for a trawler. Frantically, I had to put both engines full ahead and we missed the trawler by just two feet. Half the crew nearly fell over with the sudden change of direction, and then it was the turn of those ashore to laugh at us.

'Later we learned that the cow had fallen in when being loaded aboard a ship. The vet wrote to thank us, and say that both the cow and her new calf were all right.'

Much more worrying was the time when Tommy got lost. 'It was in the days before sophisticated direction-finding equipment came in, when most coxes only used to know their own patches well and found things very difficult when out of sight of land. We only went by compass, guess and by God.

'Along with the Aldeburgh and Harwich boats, we were called out when two US Airforce planes collided and ditched, thirty-five miles south-east. A fishing boat had picked up one pilot and we were to search for the other.

'We left at midnight, and I'd been up all night before on the pilot boat, of which I was cox before my son. We only did 8½ knots, so at best it would have been over four hours before we got there, but with the tide against us it took 5½ hours.

'On arrival we started the "expanded box" search while the other boats worked different areas. Eventually we picked up some fuselage debris and they sent out a big chopper which dropped a paramedic into the sea and he came to see us. They wanted all the bits, and from the human skin on the wreckage they were later able to confirm that the pilot was dead.

'At dusk the Gorleston boat was sent to relieve us. As I turned for home the weather was worsening, with an imminent gale from the north-east. By then it seemed as if I'd been up for ages, so it wasn't funny when both the radio and radar packed up and all I had to go by was the compass. But unfortunately, I hadn't noticed that with all the bang-bang the compass had jumped over in the gimbals. Then, unbelievably, both engines stopped and we were all over the place.

'The only way to tell how much fuel was left in the tanks was to dip them, but this wasn't possible with the sea washing over us. Then I worked out that I could run both the diesels off one tank, but when we got going I realised we had only a third of a tank left.

'Then I saw a flash and thought it was the three-flash of the Shipwash light vessel, and went towards it because I knew they had the same fuel as us. But when we got there I saw it was the Smith's Knowle light vessel and we couldn't get alongside because it was too rough. It was now mid-morning and we were still thirty miles out, but at least I had a position. All I could do was ease down with the flood and hope for the best. Meanwhile they'd sent a plane out to search for us as we had no radio and we'd "gone missing".

'But we did get in all right, and when I put the dipstick in the tanks one was bone dry and the other had only about a gallon left. A refuelling tanker came down and put eighty-three gallons in each—but when I put the dipstick in again, one tank was still bone dry. The RNLI told us to start lifting the deck off, and when we did we saw that the missing fuel was slopping about in the bilges. We discovered that someone had been "persuaded" to do a bit of "price-cutting" and had fitted old aircraft tanks whose seams had opened up with all the pounding we'd had.

'By 5pm new tanks had been fitted, we'd undergone trials, and were fully operational. That's Institution engineers for you! Not many firms could match that.'

But clearly any boat is only as good as its skipper, and there is no doubt that they do not come better than that old sea-dog Tommy Knott.

FROM THE ARCHIVES

The Fishermen's Church

THERE is in Lowestoft a curious church known as the 'Fishermen's Church', where every year a special service of thanksgiving is held for the safety of those who go down to the sea in ships. At this service, the chancel and pulpit are decorated with festoons of fish, while baskets, nets, trawl-ropes and other necessaries of the profession testify to the character of its congregation.

From Christopher Marlowe's *People and Places in Marshland* (1927)

Poor But Contented

MY home as a boy was in a quaint old fishing village close to the edge of the North Kent marshes. The place had an old, irregular look; one would think its inhabitants had begun building from the shore inland to a certain point, and then come back and finished along the water's edge.

The top rooms of the houses generally projected over the pavements—somewhat savouring of Shakespearian—with queer gables, which were ornamented with grotesque figures. By the water stood old mills, warehouses, and shipyards, all having a decayed look. That business of some kind had been once carried on there, the old wharves and fine houses showed, but when that time was no one about the place in my time knew. It was entirely isolated from any other town or village, and railroads and steamboats were things known only by name to the general community. Nearly all the people got their living on the water. Poor they were, but a contented lot, and, as the world runs, honest. Now and again it would be gently hinted that they smuggled—who can say? The virtuous have enemies; they, perhaps, had theirs. One thing I can testify—if at any time a little medicine was needed, it was sure to come out of a very short-necked, dark-green bottle holding more than a pint, and that medicine was certainly made in Holland.

From W. Halliday's *Book of Migratory Birds* (1909)

114

GUARDIAN OF THE GANNETS

FRED MARR

BOATMAN TO THE BASS ROCK
AND LOBSTER FISHERMAN OF LOTHIAN

North Berwick fishermen, circa 1880. Pictured right is Fred's great uncle,
James ('Daddy') Marr, who was harbour master for over sixty years

WHEREAS previous generations of his fishing family only occasionally glanced at the gannet to help find the shoals, Fred Marr has come to rely on the bird to make a living. Just three miles off his North Berwick home lies the spectacular Bass Rock, fortress for seabirds of all types, but most importantly home to Britain's oldest-known gannet colony. Every year thousands of twitchers and tourists flock to this wonder of the bird world, but the only way they can get a close look is from aboard Fred's boat. Not surprisingly, his craft is called the *Sula*, after the gannet's Latin name, *Sula bassana*, the second word of which derives from the Bass Rock itself.

Yet the birds have not suffered through the rise of tourism. On the contrary, over the first twenty years of Fred's passenger trips, the number of Bass gannets increased from some 9,000 to over 50,000, thanks mostly to his care and management. Indeed, the Dalrymples, who have owned the rock since 1706, could have no finer guardian of the gannets. Fred Marr is from that fine old school of conservationists, men always ready to intervene with practical measures such as predator control rather than let nature take an often undesirable course.

Records reveal that Fred's family has lived at North Berwick and earned a living from the sea since 1791, probably even earlier. The concentration has been on fishing, but some of his ancestors have been pilots, and Fred's great uncle—James 'Daddy' Marr, who died in 1937 aged ninety-seven, was harbourmaster for over sixty years.

Born on 14 October 1923 and one of two children, Fred was christened Alfred William. But his father too was called Alfred, leading to some confusion, so they split the name between them and Marr senior became known as Alf, while Marr junior was dubbed Fred.

During Fred's younger days, North Berwick was 'chock-a-block with folk in summer, especially out from Edinburgh—just twenty-two miles away, but it completely changed with the advent of the package holiday. There used to be three passenger boats here, but now my son Chris and me run the only one.

'Granny once had a fish and chip shop here, and right outside it the buses left for Haddington and Dunbar. Many people would leave a standing order with her and collect it when catching the bus back, at the end of their day out. Country people used to rely on the bus in these (those) days.

'You could get a huge fish and chips for sixpence then. Haddock has always been the most popular fish in Scotland, but Granny also sold whiting and codling. No one up here has ever bothered with fish like skate and catfish, and all those other queer things you eat down south.

'Granny's fish were all caught by father. He had three mile of line with a hook every eighteen inches. The place was teeming with fish. No one was allowed to trawl then. Before my lifetime there were a lot more fishing boats here, and there were quite a few when I was a boy, but now there are only five and the harbour's full of yachts.'

When he was not fishing or sailing—always a great family interest—young Fred earned a few shillings carrying clubs for golfers. 'Lots of local boys and men did this because we had many visitors from the south, especially London. We even had a couple of Prime Ministers. They also came up for the grouse, and sometimes I went beating on the moor. I also helped with all the rowing boats which were hired out then.

'There was no such thing as pocket money in those days. If you knew your folk didn't have the money you didn't expect it. You learnt to make your own amusement.' And like all children, young Fred occasionally acted the dare-devil. 'At the time of the King's jubilee celebrations in 1935, when they built a big bonfire on top of the Law [the 612ft hill overlooking the town], us kids rolled tyres down. They finished up in the marsh at the bottom.'

Fred was bright enough but did not like going to the local school and left at the age of fourteen to become an apprentice printer for a local company. 'Unfortunately the

Successful catch: a young Fred removes a couple of lobsters from one of his home-made creels

trade went down when the war started so I was paid off. Then I worked in a butcher's shop for several years, and then for a grocer.

'I couldn't go in the Army because I had been passed grade 4 with a heart murmur, so I joined the NAAFI. When the invasion was comin' up they asked for volunteers and I went to Tweseldown racecourse, near Aldershot. But they wouldn't take me overseas and eventually I went back to the NAAFI in Scotland.

'In 1944 I married Joan, who came from Dunbar. After the war I had no intention of going into fishing, but with the food shortage prices had jumped, and fish numbers were up because the ground had had a rest. So I started with Father in 1945, mostly on the lobsters.'

The first boat Fred worked was the *Nora*—'a 24ft Fifie double-ender with a single-cylinder Kelvin petroleum/paraffin engine. She also carried a dipping lugsail, but this was only used on long trips. Every time you went about you had to take down the sail and take it round the other side of the mast. *Nora* was built in 1917 and I believe she's still going strong. Before my father sold her I had the *Girl Pat* built.'

With lobsters plentiful after the war, Fred and his father ran about a hundred creels and later built up to two hundred. 'Even when you could take the spawn lobsters we put them back. One day we had a hundred lobsters out of ninety-six creels after the lobster had renewed their shell. You could haul creel three times a day and always get good catches. But then you could pick and choose where you went, and we were always careful to rest the ground.

'We've always used the traditional Scottish creel as opposed to the Cornish beehive creel. In the winter we have to operate in deeper water to save the gear being smashed up. But strangely, in recent years they've been catching more lobsters inshore in winter. In the old days we never even thought of doing that.

'Originally our creels were made from three-year-old ash, which I had to bend and season in shape. When a rod was pushed through the creel base its end was split, and a wedge held it in place. Later we went on to penang cane and electric drills, which made life much easier. Now even cane is hard to get, as most people use plastic. But even the strongest creels get broken. We had one-inch ash rods smashed in a big sea, even when set as deep as sixty feet.

'Only a few lobsters were sold locally. Most were sent down to Manchester or Billingsgate by rail, but that was a dodgy business in hot weather. You only had to miss one connection and lots would be dead. Also, the dealer would complain that some of those still alive were 'sleepy', and that by the time he sent them out to his customers they, too, would be dead. But you just had to believe them.

'We stored the lobsters in hinged wooden boxes in the sea and you had to have a bit of depth to the water so that they didn't suffocate when the water warmed up. We sent them off as often as three times a week in summer, but once a week in winter. We packed them in dry sawdust, but in winter, when it was cool, all you needed was layers of tangle [seaweed]. Then lobsters could last as long as a couple of weeks provided their gills were moist. One of the best things for them was coaldust. Some of the old fellers used to put lobsters—and peeler crabs—in the coal cellar to revive them.

The puffin: one of the great crowd-pullers on Fred's patch

'When prices were at a maximum during the war, lobsters fetched 5 shillings a pound in winter and half-a-crown in summer. Pre-war they only made 9d a pound, and crabs were a shilling a dozen. Nowadays you can get up to £6 a pound near Christmas, when lobsters are scarce. But everybody wants a sort of medium size, about 1¼ to 1½lb, and some places have a job getting rid of the big stuff. The largest I ever had weighed 7½lb.

'When herring were cheap we bought boxes from the market to bait the creels. There was also plenty of fresh mackerel in summer and we'd salt some for winter use. When mackerel's been in the brine for a while it goes quite golden with all the oil, and that's what you want to attract the lobster. But crabs are the fussy ones: they like fresh bait. Quite frankly, I often wonder what the lobsters go in the creel for. Sometimes you catch a big lobster and the bait's hardly touched. But the little crabs are a real nuisance: you can get two dozen in a creel, with only a couple of marketable size, and you have to spend ages fishing them out.

'Sometimes you get codling in the creel and they can be used for bait. And if you're really stuck you can even use crab shell. Other fish which go in the creel after the bait include flatfish and conger eels. We gave some congers to Edinburgh Zoo. One I had was 15lb and it was killed by a smaller one in the creel. But another boat had one much larger—when I tried to span it, my hands only went halfway round the body.'

Despite fishing for lobsters in all weathers, Fred only ever fell overboard once. 'We were on the old *Nora* and I leaned on a bit of plank that wasn't well

Happy release: Fred helps one of the many gannets which get entangled in discarded fishing line

supported. Luckily I managed to grab hold of the side of the boat and didn't go into the propeller. The funny thing is I was smokin' a pipe when I went over, and still smokin' it when I got back in. I've lost a few pipes over the side in my time. Father was a pipe smoker, too, and I just took over from him.

'You had to be careful not to fall in with the old heavy sea boots on. And when I was a youngster the old boys still had leather thigh boots and oilskins that went so hard you were all thumbs trying to do them up. We used to have oilskin frocks that came down just below the knee, but a few fellers got caught up in the winches, and they were murder in hot, clammy weather.'

There was only one occasion when Fred could not get into harbour after a fishing trip. 'About four years ago I came back from the lobsters at high water and couldn't even look at the pier with the seas breaking. So I had to put in further up the firth, at Port Seton, fourteen miles away. But once you get round the corner, at Gullane, it's a different world with the shelter.

'The worst winter we had was 1947, when the snow lay for twelve weeks, from January to March. We had a south-easterly gale about once a week and I've never known a year like it for losing gear. That was when we used tarred sisal rope, which got all twisted, and strained easily. We were forever replacing things, and were not catching much either—we even had to cash insurance policies and savings certificates to keep going.'

In 1972 Fred started to take people out to see the Bass Rock and its gannets. 'I charged about seven bob a time in old money and *Sula 1* could take up to forty-eight people. Later I took on *Sula 2*, which is licensed for seventy-one passengers, and now I also take in Craigleith Island because everybody wants to see the puffins and there aren't many on Bass. But you can't see puffins all the time. They arrive in March to breed, and are all gone by about 20 August. Those on Craigleith have been helped a bit by the arrival of Bass mallow in about 1980. When the birds arrive back at their nest burrows with beakfuls of fish they usually lose some to the gulls, but now they have more protection as they drop through the mallow to their burrows. Before that the Bass mallow had been peculiar to the Bass Rock.'

In 1993 the fare for Fred's 1¼-hour boat trip was just £3.40 for adults, and half-price for children, which was very reasonable considering the hefty overheads such as insurance. 'And since that ferry disaster on the Thames there's been reams of bumf to fill in. The Department of Transport want £300 before they even come out for their annual inspection.'

Fred operates his passenger boat from 1 April to 31 October only, and at the height of the season no more than three trips a day are made; he used to do up to five when it was just to the Bass. Furthermore, even within the season the weather is unpredictable, especially early and late. When I went out, on 8 April, it was Fred's first sailing for seven days. Not surprisingly, as we went down to

Fred heads for home after another successful tourist trip around the Bass Rock

Gannet and young

the boat a visitor asked: 'Do you only go out on Wednesdays?' There had been plenty of people wanting to go, especially with the Easter holiday, but the sea had been too rough. 'It's not just a case of waiting for the sun. The swells are very awkward and you can't take any risks with people's lives.'

In the old days any boat could land on Bass, but today Fred's is the only one allowed to do so. Not surprisingly, when it was a free-for-all 'the birds used to be scared off a lot and the gulls got their eggs. But now it's well controlled, landings are rare, and there's an average increase in the gannet population of three to four per cent a year. The RSPB have tried to buy the island twice, but it couldn't be better run than it is now. Sir Hugh is very proud of his rock.'

There is no warden on the Bass, but regular checks are made by Fred and his son Chris. 'The lighthouse is automated now, but I always remember when the keepers came off because it was the day of the Lockerbie plane disaster.

'I used to take mail out to the lightmen, as well as other things when they ran out. They had a Blondin wire for heavin' stuff up. The principal said it was the best rock light he'd been on. But that was before the helicopter pad was built, when they had six weeks on and two weeks off. I never thought I'd see the day there were no men out there. Now the light's been downgraded and only has a range of nine miles, so it looks like a wee torch when it's a bit hazy. The trouble is, nobody wants to pay for lighthouses now ships have got all these modern aids.

'The Bass light was built low down because there is a ready-made ledge there for easy access and the top of the island is often shrouded in low cloud. In any case there was already a good light on the nearby Isle of May and between them they covered all directions. The May light used to take three ton of coal a night, and they say that one of the keepers was asphyxiated by the fumes.

'Robert Louis Stevenson's father was joint-engineer to the Board of Northern Lighthouses. The novelist was a native of Edinburgh and he used to stay here in North Berwick for his holidays. Fidra, 2½ miles over there, is supposed to be where he got the idea for "Treasure Island".

'The Bass lightkeepers used to have a market garden but found it almost impossible to keep up when someone introduced rabbits, thinking it was a good idea to have "meat on the hoof". But the rabbits died out with myxomatosis. They reckon gulls brought the infected fleas from the mainland.

'One thing the lightkeepers certainly didn't expect was to find a seal right outside their door. One had climbed all the way up the steps to the base of the tower and the principal tripped over it when he stepped outside.'

But there were buildings on the Bass long before a light was built. St Baldred, a disciple of St Kentigern, sought refuge there, and ruins remain of the fortress built by the Lauder family in the early fourteenth century. With sheer cliffs rising to 350ft around much of its one-mile circumference, the Bass—the basalt core of an old volcano—was already almost impregnable. From 1691 to 1694 a Jacobite garrison, aided by the French, held the rock for James II against the forces of William III. It took a long naval blockade to bring about their surrender.

The same precipitous sides which made a natural fortress are known to have attracted gannets since the days of William the Conqueror. But as the bird population has returned to garrison strength so the jockeying for best position has increased. Mortality is as high as seventy per cent among young gannets which fall or get pushed off narrow ledges before due time.

Fred explained: 'With the increase they have been forced to go up and down for sites and the young, which are up to 3lb heavier than their parents, have little room. A lot of them face into the cliff and fall off if they flap too vigorously. I've even seen them

Sandwich terns

knock another down when they tumble. But gannets have a tremendous resilience. Once a young one smacked down 250ft into the water right next to my boat, but before I could pick it up it simply shook itself and paddled away.

'Some get airborne OK and may make a successful first flight of a mile or so. But even then they are not safe because they must perfect their fishing technique before burning up their fat reserves or die of starvation. Over the years I've had to bring a lot home and look after them in the garden. That's OK as long as there's plenty of mackerel, but other fish, such as whiting, don't have the nutritional value. Despite all this, I still hope to see the rock covered by gannets before I go to the great beyond.

'Everyone loves watching the gannets. They have a special way of standing on the wind. It's not unusual for people to stay on the boat and go back round again for another trip, they're so impressed by the birds. There's one German chap regularly brings a party birdwatching in Britain and he says: "I always save the Bass till last. I daren't show this first as nothing else could live up to it."'

Because the gannet is such a spectacular plunge-diver it doesn't have any nostrils and breathes through its open beak, which makes it difficult to hold when help is required, as Fred knows only too well.

'The males often get entangled in bits of discarded net when gathering nest material along the tideline. The trouble is these trawlers just cut out badly torn pieces and chuck them overboard. It can drive you daft trying to catch the snared birds. In fact it's best if they're well netted so that you can get them with the boat hook. But when you free them you don't get any thanks for it. Not only are their beaks like vices but sharp, too, with serrations to hold the fish, so they can easily take a strip of skin off your hand as they pull away.

'Once I saw this gannet with yards and yards of seaweed looped around its beak and trailing away, and it couldn't get it off. I soon realised that the weed was caught around fishing line.'

The gannet's powerful beak is a formidable fish-catcher and the saying 'hungry as a gannet' is entirely appropriate. Fred has often seen the bird eat two whole mackerel in quick succession. 'Sometimes you can see the tail of the second one sticking out of the bird's mouth, and I have even seen one try to gobble three in a row. Also, once I threw a 2½lb codling overboard to see how they would cope with it. The first gannet that tried couldn't manage, but the second just gave one or two shakes and down the fish went. They always eat a fish head first, so that the gills don't stick.'

There is no doubt that gannets are also excellent fish finders, and in their constant search for food are attracted to anything else in the water. 'Last August [1992] Chris pointed to a lot of gannets apparently fishing, and the nearer we went there were more and more. But it was a school of dolphins which had attracted them and I should think half the population of the rock followed them for about four or five miles. Gannets always investigate anything unusual and I don't suppose most of them had ever seen a dolphin before.

'Another time we went to see what they were attracted to and it was the periscope of a submarine going up and down in the water. And there was a time

The Bass Rock: once a prison, now an important gannet stronghold

when they gathered round an empty canoe—later we discovered that the owner had drowned up the firth.'

Fred still remembers the first time he saw some dolphins. 'I spotted a group of about fifty when I was thirteen and out fishing on my own in a 10ft dinghy. They were headed towards me so I took my boots off in a hurry because I visualised one would land in the boat and sink me. But fortunately the party split and went each side. I've also seen a few whales in my time, but the big ones only twice.

'Up to World War 1 the young gannets themselves were harvested. There were special ovens for them at Canty Bay, which is the nearest point on the mainland. They've gone now, but you can still see the chimneys where the birds were processed. Most were eaten, but the main interest was in their fat, especially that of the young, which they need to live off when the fishing is bad. One bird can yield ¾lb of oil, which was used for all sorts of things from lubricating cartwheels, machines and boots to curing gout and other ailments. The processing plant must have smelt awful because the gannet has a strong odour. In the old days the local minister was given twelve gannets a year as part of his stipend.'

Fortunately, the gannets themselves are not too troubled by oil polluting the environment. Fred has picked up a few affected birds 'which generally die despite my efforts because they've ingested the oil while preening. But they're not affected so much as other seabirds, such as razorbills and guillemots, because they don't spend much time on the water. They just dive and get straight off.'

Dolphins: when Fred was 13 he was startled by a group of about fifty

In protecting the gannets and other seabirds Fred has become extremely anti-gull. But he is far from alone in this. In many areas gull populations have multiplied to such an extent that even conservation organisations have had to control them.

'On Lamb Island there used to be a strong colony of arctic and common terns, but the gulls chased them off in the wartime. Then the terns, including sandwich and roseate, got well established on Fidra and when the RSPB bought that island they had to cull the gulls there.

'One time the Nature Conservancy poisoned 18,000 gulls in one day on the Isle of May out there. They were very careful and put the poison right next to each nest to make sure that no other bird would take it. However, some of the dead gulls washed ashore on the mainland and the Conservancy got into a panic, so they reduced the strength of the poison in case any dogs ate the birds. I've no time for gulls. They take or kill so many chicks and eggs of other birds.'

Years ago, Fred was one of the people who regularly collected gulls' eggs from Craigleith Island and sold them locally for food. 'There was any amount of them because the birds just kept on laying if you kept gathering. You could take thirty or forty dozen a day if you wished, though getting them off and landing with them was another matter because they were so fragile, and there was no proper landing stage there, only slippery rocks covered in green algae.

'As youngsters, we used to have egg fights on Craigleith. Woe betide anyone who went under the east side of the cliff while the eggs were being gathered!

'Once I bent down to pick up these three eggs and must have straightened up a bit quick because this divebombing gull hit me square in the back of the head. At the same time I heard this squelching noise and felt all this hot mud down my neck when he dropped his load. Well, I'd heard of humans doing their stuff when frightened, but never a gull!

'The lightkeepers on Bass had a few gulls' eggs too, but there weren't nearly so many there. They kept the spare eggs in a tank of lime water until the fresh ones came round again.'

On another occasion it was one of Fred's passengers who was surprised by a 'message from above', but then he did deserve it. 'Just occasionally we've had to drop someone off on the Bass for a pee when they've been in the pub just before coming on board.

Most of Fred's passengers have been well behaved

But this day there was a bus trip in from Glasgow and this man and two women were really drunk. They were a very rough lot and when they got on board they had half a bottle of whisky and cans of beer with them. And with all the noise they made, the others could hardly hear what I was saying over the microphone.

'But then a gannet came to the rescue and dropped a load of dirty brown stuff all over the front of this man's jacket. And it can really burn, just like lime. The drunk said to me: "Hey Mac, what about the gear?" But by then I was so annoyed by him I just replied: "What do you want me to do, put nappies on it?" After that he soon quietened down. Since then we've never had any other real troublemakers, though some of the school parties aren't very well controlled.'

Fred's most unexpected passenger was the Reverend Ian Paisley. 'He just turned up on my doorstep with his entourage and said he was going round all the places where the Covenanters had been martyred, such as the Bass, and was taking a stone from each to build a church in Northern Ireland.'

An equally famous passenger was David Bellamy, the extrovert presenter of television nature programmes. 'I've taken him out twice to make films. Once they wanted a shot of me fishing, but they didn't want to take any chances and brought a load of fish from the market so that I could stick one on my hook. "I can't do that", I said, but they weren't bothered: they thought most viewers wouldn't know the difference.

'Over the years we've had all the TV people out here, even one crew from Japan who wanted to make a film about someone who was shipwrecked and ate albatrosses. I told them we only had gannets, but they too didn't seem bothered. I was really surprised that they couldn't find an island with albatrosses on.

'The odd thing is they went to so much trouble to get everything else right. They even brought special branches all the way from Japan and had a model gannet made, not to mention a life-size dummy of a man in a loincloth, which they tossed over the cliff to mimic a suicide which took place. I happened to be nearby when they did this and it looked very realistic. I picked the dummy up, too, and we had a bit of fun with it in the town.

'I think the person who gained most from the Japanese visit was the owner of the local woollen shop. She said to me: "I hope they get more bad days when they can't film. When it was raining they came in here and just about cleaned me out because clothes prices are so much lower than in Japan."'

Another group of passengers who surprised Fred were nuns. 'The Dalrymples gave them the big house which they used to have in North Berwick. Some of them were quite old, but even they were quite nimble when it came to getting off the boat.

'There was a time when I was coming back from Fidra and I passed a boatload of kids with two nuns on the way out. Well, in the old days fishermen thought meeting nuns brought bad luck, and to get rid of it you had to turn your bonnet (cap) round, which I did for fun. Later on, I saw the skipper who took the nuns out and he told me that one of them had said: "That's the second time I've seen someone turn their hat round today. Why do they do that?"

'There were always plenty of other superstitions in the area. If you wanted to avoid bad luck you should never say the word salmon while at sea. They were always called "the red fellers". Likewise, pigs had to be called "curly tails" and rats "longtails". And you should never whistle because that's like whistling up too much wind and goes back to the days of working sailboats. But I'm not superstitious: I'm a great believer in fate.'

Fortunately for gannets, fate dictated that Fred Marr would become guardian of the Bass Rock. Today few people know more about the folklore and natural history of Britain's seabirds, whether it's the fact that the guillemot is called the 'ooyah bird' because it is distressed when laying such a large egg; or that no two guillemot eggs are said to have the same markings. 'They say all the different patterns are so that the parents can tell their own eggs, but how they do that when they're covered in white droppings I do not know!'

Birds have been the focus of Fred's hobby, too. 'I've made quite a few models, especially blue tits on coconut. But once I used polystyrene for the coconut and my friend hung it up in his porch. After a while he phoned up and said: "You'll need to send me some more 'coconut'". I can imagine what the birds were saying as they spat it out.

'But the gannets have always been my favourites and I specially like to see the joy on folk's faces when I take them out and they see the birds on the Bass for the first time. There's no doubt that my work's my real hobby. I have no plans to retire.'

FROM THE ARCHIVES

Frequented By Soland Geese

THE Bass lies about one mile from the shore, a rock of stupendous height, the top on the south side conic; the other overhangs the sea in a most tremendous manner. The castle, once the state prison of Scotland, now neglected, lies close to the edge of the precipice facing the little village of Castleton. This rock is frequented by gannets or soland geese and kittiwakes or gulls, both of which are farmed here.

From William Camden's *Britannia* (1586, revised 1789)

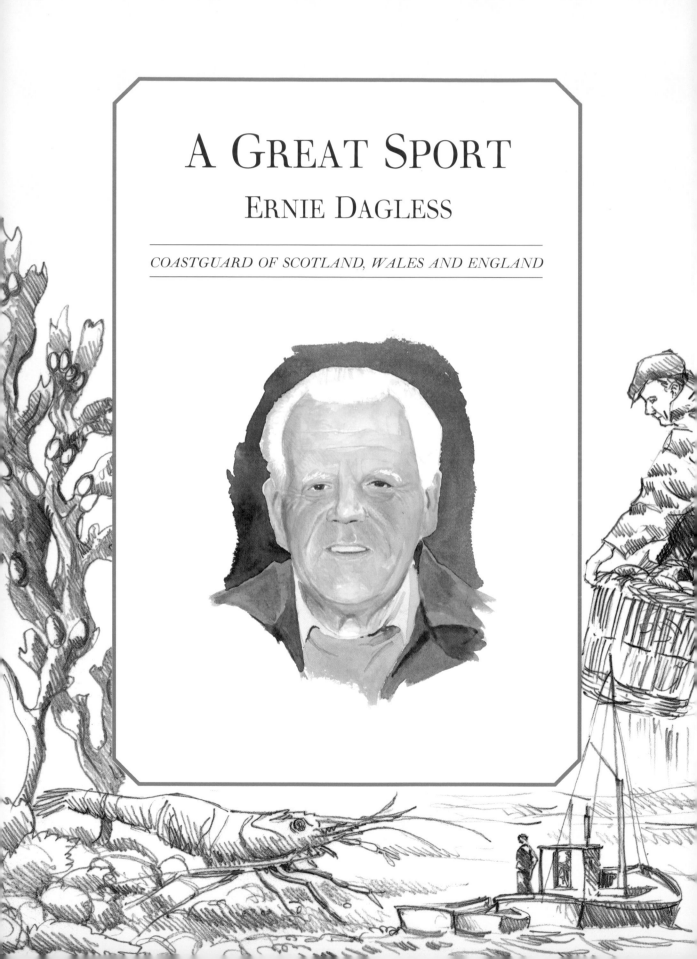

A Great Sport

Ernie Dagless

Coastguard of Scotland, Wales and England

'There's so much wildlife, with magnificent stags on the coasts'

HAVING been a keen rugby player for the South of Scotland, and later an enthusiastic rock climber, Ernie Dagless was always prepared to 'have a go'. So it is not surprising that he ended up with a couple of bravery awards. But at the same time he never lost his sense of humour, an essential attribute for anyone whose frequent dealings with disaster could easily induce depression.

Ernest William Dagless was born on 3 September 1932 at Peebles, 'from where a lot of guys went away to sea.' But he came from a soldiering family, his father having been in the Royal Scots, and his grandfather and great-grandfather in the Royal Scots Fusiliers.

One of five boys, Ernie went to India at the age of three when his father was posted to Lahore. He had just started school there when the family moved to Hong Kong, and Christmas 1937–8 was spent at sea on the way back home to the barracks at Glencrose, near Peebles. 'But even at that age I was never seasick, even when it was really rough.'

In 1946 fourteen-year-old Ernie reluctantly had to give up his place in the scrum to accompany his major father back to India. But that visit was relatively short because the family returned home the following year when India gained independence. 'On the way I was very impressed by the destroyers we saw. I thought—they move about and see the world, whereas the Army often gets stuck in one place for years. Also, I would have hated to have joined the old man's regiment and had to live up to him.

'So I joined the Royal Navy in 1948, at HMS *Bruce*, Fife. I went to *Ganges*, where I was "Boy 2nd Class", though my mother never believed that. Eventually I joined the aircraft carrier *Glory*, and then spent most of 1950 in East Grinstead hospital having skin grafts on my back and legs: I was badly burnt when I was on the signal lamp and a Firefly with one wheel up crash-landed on deck.'

In 1951 Ernie joined the submarine service, becoming leading signalman in

A sense of humour has helped Ernie through difficult times

1953 and yeoman of signals in 1955, the year in which he married. 'But in 1956 my leg started playing up. There was no way I wanted to come out the Navy as my future looked good, but they discharged me as below physical standard. Yet they'd soon have had me back if there was a war!'

From 1956 to 1963 Ernie was a crane driver at the Corby steelworks, in Northamptonshire. From 1959 he was also in the Royal Naval Reserve, becoming chief yeoman and then sub-lieutenant communications, 'which involved one or two nights a week and a lot of weekends. I was also still playing rugby—for the very successful works team Stewarts and Lloyd's, Corby.'

It was in 1962 that chance changed the course of Ernie's life. 'I was on a fortnight's RNR training when this chap suggested I should consider joining the Coastguard. But I needed a bit of persuasion as I was earning good money at the steelworks, so there would be a big drop in pay, and I would have to live in a coastguard's house. But I did go for interview, after swapping shifts so that no one would know what I was up to—good jobs were to be valued then. And in due course I received a letter saying I was accepted, but there were fifteen people ahead of me!

'Then I had a bit of luck which enabled me to jump the queue. A letter informed me that there would be a vacancy at Spurn Head, Humberside, and as it was also a Lloyd's signal station my experience would be highly valued there. So I took it.

'The first night I was there with my wife and two kids and we were dead beat when we turned in after the move. Then at 1am there was this God-awful bang— a maroon going off. I shot out of bed, looked out, saw all the station lights come on and a lorry drawing up. The nearest thing to hand was my old battledress, so I pulled this on and went down to help. There was an MFV (motor fishing vessel) under the cliff. We put a line aboard it with a rocket and then the Humber lifeboat hauled the boat off. That was my first-night introduction to the service.

'In those days we had no special training beforehand. You did your proficiency test after nine months, during which you were instructed by your station officer and colleagues. But nobody had a better start than me: my colleagues were magic, and everybody always jumped to help. I'm very proud of the service, but we've never had the glory.'

It was at Spurn Head in 1966 that Ernie first had the opportunity to show his mettle, but at the same time he was in for a great surprise. 'An aircraft had crashed, and when we got up to the Warren the tide was at ebb point, so we had to act fast. It was one lunchtime in April and there were plenty of people about.

In 1964 coastguard
equipment was much more
basic, including the
megaphone. Pictured (l to r)
are: Ernie, Bill Strachan
and Robbie Sowerby

Ernie assumed that the two men were from the crashed plane

So I got the tow-ropes from all the cars, tied the lot together, stripped down to my underpants and swam some eighty yards out with the line.

'Two guys in a single-engine Auster had been skylarking and a wingtip had hit the water, which was choppy. By the time I got out there the plane had sunk, but there were two men in the water. I held them both and swam back to shore, but soon after we got there I discovered that one of them hadn't even been on the plane. When it crashed he had been fishing nearby, so he had grabbed a plank— because he was only a weak swimmer—and had bravely gone out to help. Sadly, the real pilot drowned; his body was recovered a week later. The local police got the story and put up the fisherman and me for the Royal Humane Society citation.'

It was also in Yorkshire, 'where life was either hectic or humdrum', that Ernie experienced a most amusing episode. 'During the late summer very little happened other than maintaining the watch or carrying out station duties. But our station officer—a Yorkshire character if ever there was one—broke the routine by announcing that we had been invited to give a demonstration of the rescue gear at a huge garden fête in aid of local charities.

'It took more than us three volunteers to rig a complete breeches-buoy and hawser rapidly, so it seemed common sense to enlist the aid of the Scouts, who were also performing. We arranged for them to pull on the whips and so on, and for some to be in the selected large oak tree. Rehearsals were basic, but the lads were enthusiastic and the day dawned bright.

'However, old Bill, the station officer, had planned some special effects. As we were well inland, he thought it OK to give the lads in the tree a red, hand-held flare which they would light to start the demonstration.

*Gallantry certificate
awarded to Ernie in 1966*

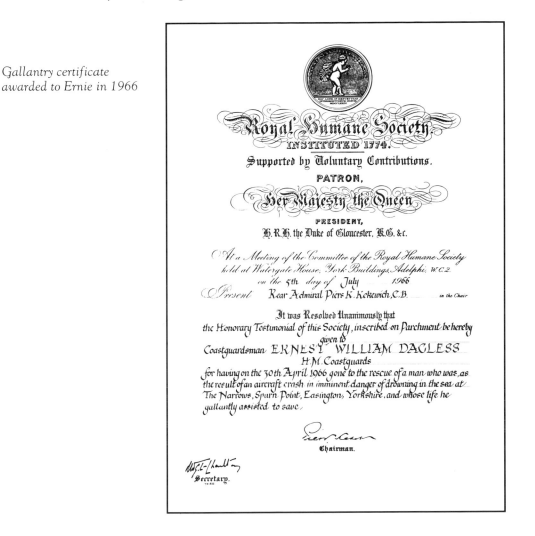

'Using a megaphone like a practised fairground barker, Bill quickly aroused interest and, after the burning of the flare, ten lads were quickly brought to safety by the breeches-buoy. And all the while the band of the Yorkshire Light Infantry played gently in the background.

'This drew a big round of applause and should have been perfect note to end on—but no, old Bill had the bit between his teeth *and* a captive audience. In any case, we were a little in hand for time. So Bill produced from our ex-Army Land Rover some parachute flares, and invited the enthralled gathering to observe that they burned with an orange-white sort of glow, so that if ever they saw one at the seaside they would not confuse it with a red distress flare.

Rock-climbing demonstration by Ernie at the Coastguard training school, Brixham, 1974

'But yet more applause deserved something bigger, and even better. So, reaching further into the depths of the vehicle, Bill unearthed an old galvanised bucket and three orange smoke canisters. Informing the audience that this was a daylight distress signal, he broke open the canisters and lit them with a big, heavy lifeboat match. Immediately a dense pall of smoke billowed down the field. Then, to our horror, the wind veered towards the assembly.

'The first victims were the band. Engulfed in the orange fog, only the end of the odd trombone or trumpet was occasionally visible, and the strains of the Emperor Waltz tailed away in a fit of coughing and profanity. Like Frankenstein's monster, out of control the fog swept into the tea marquee, depositing a rich orange powder on the cakes, sandwiches and trifles as well as every member of the public that it came in contact with.

'The screams and roars of rage broke the paralysis that gripped us, and I swear that if there was an Olympic record for unrigging and stowing gear, we broke it. As we took off down the field the first multi-coloured group burst out of the smoke, heading in our direction. But in four-wheeled drive we made the gate before them and headed home. Visibly shaken, old Bill spoke just once on the way: "By gaw, it's a good job I got them to sign the form of indemnity."

'Twelve months later I met old Bill studying the local paper in the square, when I stopped at the village shop to buy some cigarettes before going on watch. Shaking his head in disbelief, he declared: "I see they had yon fête at the Hall again, but they never asked us this year!"'

In 1968, Ernie transferred to The Mumbles, where he was awarded the RSPCA certificate of merit for a most unusual rescue. 'And you have to remember that anything we do for animals is voluntary; but it's good training, and often stops owners making silly rescue attempts.

'Like the Spurn plane crash, this event happened just when I came back from shopping, in October 1970. The boss said: "Fancy a job inland? A Jack Russell's gone down a disused mineshaft and the dog means a lot to the farmer." So off we went—three of us—to Capel Hendre, near Ammanford, Carmarthenshire.

'When we got to the shaft we found that it had about a foot of concrete over it, but there were a lot of people gathered round and one chap offered to get his pneumatic drill. Then, with the dog still barking away, we discovered that the concrete was reinforced with railway track. But the chap with the drill said that he also had an acetylene torch, and off he went to get it.

'We soon had a hole big enough to get through. The station officer said he'd go, but he wasn't getting any younger so Dick Slaney and me tossed for it. Dick won, and went down to the dog while I shone a torch from a little way in, and the RSPCA man dropped a basket down. But then I could see that Dick was swaying about in the foul air, so I said, "Forget the dog, get him out first". Luckily Dick was all right as soon as he was back up in the fresh air; and after that we soon had the dog up, too. The 150ft-deep mine, at Pencae Farm, had been shut for a century and there was hardly any oxygen at the bottom.

'The farmer who owned the dog said: "How much do I owe you?" But of course we said: "Nothing"; the satisfaction was enough. But he insisted on taking us back for the biggest farmhouse tea you've ever seen. And when we left for home we had stacks of apples and about two dozen eggs each. Dick Slaney got the RSPCA bronze medal as well.'

In 1971 Ernie became the station officer at Orkney, where he encountered a particularly stormy November. 'It was indeed a black fortnight, and how no one was killed I don't know. The seas lifted the boats so high you could see under their keels.

'We still had the Icelandic fishing then, and the Danes used Kirkwall harbour. On the worst day you could lean on the wind—it was a hundred knots plus—and wires were snapping all over the place. Miraculously there was only small damage to the ships. Most of my team were dockers. Nobody argued—everybody just got on with it. Afterwards we looked at our hands and couldn't believe the knocks and cuts. But then, my generation were trained to take a calculated risk. If you didn't think you could hack it you wouldn't do it.'

From 1972 to 1976 Ernie was station officer at the brand-new coastguard training school, Brixham, followed by four years as station officer at Falmouth. In 1980 he became district officer [controller] at Stornoway, Isle of Lewis: and from 1985 to retirement in 1992 he was district officer at Portland, where his patch stretched from Exmouth to the Dorset/Hampshire border. He enjoyed every posting, but remembers the five years at Stornoway as 'among the happiest of my life. I really liked the way of life in the Western Isles, where the people were so friendly and there's so much wildlife, with magnificent stags on the coasts and great skeins of geese filling the sky.'

Wherever he went, Ernie always managed to add to his fund of amusing stories. From his training-school days he particularly remembers the lad who got his aeroplanes and helicopters mixed up. In one test the trainee wrote: 'A Nimrod has a 200ft winch wire, but you've got to be quick!'

But Ernie's favourite yarn involves the coastguard lookout at a gun-site built into the cliff, on the day when the relief went to relieve himself and was relieved to escape sudden death. 'The roof was really thick and solid, so they built a mortar into it to fire the maroons. One day, just as he was handing over the watch, coastguard Terry said: "Hold on, I'll just nip up and fire the maroons". And while he went about this the relief went to the toilet. Unfortunately, after lighting the fuse, Terry dropped a maroon down the stench pipe instead of the mortar. There was one hell of a bang as the first charge exploded in the toilet around this chap's ears. Then the delayed charge went off about twenty feet above Terry's head instead of a thousand feet up. Luckily no one was injured.'

Today, widower Ernie Dagless lives alone in the coastguard cottage which he bought at Wyke Regis. At long last he has no need to be on constant alert—but he remains a great sport as a very active member of Weymouth Golf Club, where the yarns are just as abundant.

'We could hear the dog barking 150 feet below'

FROM THE ARCHIVES

Hardy Holidaymakers

THE wind blew with a fury from the sea; it was hard to walk against it. The people in hundreds waited in their dull apartments for a lull, and when it came they poured out like hungry sheep from the fold, or like children from a school, swarming over the green slope down to the beach, to scatter far and wide over the sands. Then, in a little while, a new menacing blackness would come up out of the sea, and by and by a fresh storm of wind would send the people scuttling back into shelter. So it went on day after day.

From W. H. Hudson's *Afoot In England* (1909)

MORE MUD THAN BLOOD

FRANK HARRISON

WILDFOWLING GUIDE ON THE WASH

'I THOUGHT you had to be dead to be this cold', remarked one young man who went wildfowling for the first time. But his guide and mentor, who was three times his age, felt not a thing because most of his life had been spent ambushing geese and duck on the icy saltmarshes of eastern England.

Today, septuagenarian Frank Harrison remains as hardy and keen as ever, having notched up 121 flights in the 1992–3 season alone. But whereas the expression 'more mud than blood' has always applied to Frank's make-up, now it describes his sport, too. Wildfowl distribution has changed to such an extent that his occasional customers are more likely to return home with a bagful of ooze rather than their next roast dinner. Regulars appreciate the unpredictability of the sport.

Despite this, few are disappointed. There is so much more to wildfowling than birds in the bag. It is the sport of loners, that which truly satisfies the age-old hunter's spirit, and one which takes you as close to wilderness as you are ever likely to get in modern Britain. As Frank Harrison knows, the sight and sound of wild geese thronging in a winter sunset is reason enough to be there.

Yet this guru among marshmen was not born with buckshot in his hand. 'The only thing Father ever shot was a 4in gun on a destroyer!' Indeed, it was not until he was a strapping thirteen-year-old that a chance encounter showed him the attractions of things which honk and quack. Young Frank was among the most enthralled when, in 1935, Peter Scott gave a talk to the pupils at Spalding Grammar School. 'At the time, Scott was living nearby at Sutton Bridge lighthouse and was as mad on shooting wildfowl as he was on painting and collecting them. I used to cycle over to see him sometimes and we got on well together; but I still didn't have a gun.

'In 1939, when I was seventeen, I went over to see Peter at the lighthouse. He was going off to the Black Sea to collect some geese and I was going to ask him if I could look after his birds. But it was 3 September, the very day that war broke

Veteran of the marshes—Frank Harrison

out, and because he joined the Navy the wildfowl collection had to be dispersed. So for the time being I had to content myself with working on the land, as Father had done.'

Christened Leslie, Frank was born on 2 December 1922, at Walsoken, near Wisbech, just inside the Norfolk boundary; though after two weeks the family moved to Lutton Marsh. 'Father took a smallholding there after he came out of the Navy in 1919. It was one of many provided for ex-servicemen when the large farms were broken up. We grew anything we could.

'When I was five we moved a couple of miles to a bigger smallholding near Sutton Bridge, Lincolnshire, and that was my home till I was twenty-one. During that time I worked three horses, and that gave me the strength in me legs.'

At that time the area was far less intensively farmed and Frank recalls a wealth of wildlife. 'Wherever you went you could pick buttercups and violets, and the dykes were full of little fish, spawn, toads and frogs.' There was an abundance of birdlife too, on both inland and coastal marshes, the ideal training ground for a fowling guide.

'After school at Sutton Bridge I only went to Spalding Grammar for two years because Dad couldn't afford to send both me and my younger sister there. In the summer I used to cycle 4¼ miles each way six days a week, just to save ten bob a term. And I often had to help with the work on the smallholding during holidays.

'My sister went on to university, but I had to leave school at fourteen. I did everythin' on the smallholding, from sowing potatoes, oats and wheat, to cutting round the edges of the fields with a scythe at harvest, and yoking the horses to the binder. Nowadays many farmers just sit on their ass in a tractor.'

Although he was in a reserved occupation, Frank volunteered for the Navy in March 1942, at the age of nineteen. After training at HMS *Collingwood*, he was posted to Combined Operations, working on landing craft. 'I joined up with a friend at Long Sutton—our numbers were next to one another—and he still lives there.'

Frank modestly makes light of his part in the D-Day landings ('We were so highly trained it was just like any other manoeuvre!'), but the Mark 5 craft which

he coxswained was one of only very few that managed to beach twice that day!
'After dropping tanks and troops on the beach in the first wave of assault, we
got off. We then went alongside HMCS *Prince David*, embarked about two
hundred French Canadian troops and got them ashore too. But this time, with
falling water, we couldn't get off and had to wait for the rising tide in the
afternoon before we could refloat.

'Subsequently my wife Peg had a card to say I was missing in action, presumed
killed. Later I went to India for the Far East war and my son, born in 1944, was
two years old before I saw him.'

When Frank left the Navy in 1946, Peter Scott came to the house and asked
him to work for him, helping to establish the collection which would become the
nucleus of the Wildfowl Trust. 'It sounded very attractive, with a house and a
little car for Peg, but it meant long separation from the family, with me
accompanying Peter to places like Iceland for six months of the year; so I turned
it down. I planned to return to the land. Dad had put me down for a smallholding,
but they kept bein' let to non ex-servicemen. So I went to see my MP about it
and had one within a week.

'By then I'd been shooting for some time and I can still remember my first shot,

'The sight and sound of wild geese thronging in a winter sunset is reason enough to be there'

Frank and Peggy developed the Crown and Woolpack at Long Sutton as a mecca for wildfowlers

though I'm not sure when it was. I bagged a curlew at Wingland, by the lighthouse, using a single-barrel, bolt-action 12-bore. Later on I lent it to Jim Plumb, who kept the fish shop at Sutton Bridge, and he blew it out. It was Jim who taught Kenzie Thorpe—the legendary "wild goose man"—to paint. We fowled a lot together.'

But even the hardiest of shooters are sometimes thwarted by nature, such as in 1953 when parts of the east coast were devastated by floods, and hundreds of people lost their lives. On 30 January Frank went down to Shep White's, 'to the access point near the bombing range. Just before dark a big skein of pinkfeet dropped in on the other side of the creek, so I rang Bob Tall at Wisbech. He came out with me on the Friday and we sat on this scaffolding, which was an old bomb plotting tower four hundred yards out, and waited, for this was where the geese had dropped in the previous night. But nothing came. The birds knew what was goin' on all right.

'On the Saturday, Cyril Burbridge and his friend saw this sudden wall of water, where one tide had built on another, rushing up the creek. They 'ad to crawl along the seawall the wind was so strong. Then they had a job to get Cyril's old Ford van to start, but, with the crank handle under water, it just fired up in time to get them off.

'Just after 5pm I had a phone call from Jim Plumb, who asked me to come and fetch the kids because the water was coming in the shop and had put the fire out! But when I went over to Sutton Bridge in my 1939 Hillman I met the water in the High Street. Luckily I had waders with me and was able to carry the kids back to the car. With our lot included, we had eight kids for a week—and it was chaos!

'Later I discovered that Bob and me had been the last two up that scaffolding. The next time we went down the marsh we saw that the tower had been washed three-quarters of a mile away. No wonder the geese didn't come back.'

Snow, too, has been an occasional problem, such as the time in the early eighties when Frank was taking Dr Edward Barrington-Ward over to the Hare and Hounds, which was the access point for shooting on the River Welland. 'Fortunately we didn't get down there, as we'd have been stuck for ages. A lorry was snowed in on the A17, and at 5.30am we stopped behind it. Within minutes we could hardly open the car door. Luckily we were allowed to stay the night in a nearby nursery, but it was the following evening before we got home.

'I kept the smallholding till 1955, but there was never any chance of getting more land on top of my twenty-five acres because I'd upset the agent; so I took the Crown and Woolpack pub at Long Sutton. It was only then that wildfowling began to dominate my life. We started to take fowlers in, and soon got a good name because we knew just what they wanted, starting with a bloody great breakfast after morning flight. I had a nice write-up in *Shooting Times*, and since then I've never really needed to advertise. Some people have been coming back ever since.

'In 1960 we gave up the pub and I started to work for the civil engineers W. & C. French. Every November, till I retired from engineering at sixty-five, I handed my notice in so that I could return to the foreshore for the rest of the season. Fortunately they always took me back after shooting ended, on 20 February.'

At first the wildfowling was largely uncontrolled, with no permits or tickets, and Frank could go anywhere from the River Ouse to the River Witham, over some twenty miles. 'But that wasn't any good for the birds or the sport, with so many cowboys about, so clubs started forming; and they took control of the ground. I joined the Fenland Wildfowlers' Association and now it's all permits. I go mainly on the eight miles between the Nene and the Ouse.'

Stricter control of the sport was essential, not only to safeguard wildfowl populations—through bag restrictions and habitat preservation and management—but also to improve safety standards. The irresponsible men who took whatever they could, whenever and wherever they could, were those most likely to drown through sheer ignorance. Without local knowledge of terrain, tides and bird behaviour, a stranger would be more likely to kill himself than a few birds. Today there are many fowlers who owe their sporting success—some even their lives—to the skill of men such as Frank Harrison. In the 1950s and '60s there were five professional guides on The Wash; now there are only two.

Frank insists it's all a matter of common sense. 'You must have a compass for when it's foggy, know the tide times and never jump anythin' if you can't jump

(*Overleaf*) *'When it's raining and blowing a gale birds come driving in low'*

145

it full of water. And now it's nothing like as dangerous as it was because so much land has been drained and reclaimed. The tide used to come right into the lighthouse, but now the water is stopped by the bank constructed in 1953.'

Despite the undoubted rigours of the sport, Frank's customers have been a surprisingly mixed bag, ranging from doctors, dentists and pilots to rugby players, mechanics and porters. 'There was a psychiatrist, a racing driver who introduced me to the getaway man in the Great Train Robbery, a monk who came for three days at Christmas and stayed for eight, and a minister of the church from Cambridge who came through terrible weather on a brand new BMW motorbike. I even had a polio victim. He had such unbelievable energy, and became addicted to the sport despite having only two fingers on one hand.

'One of the most enthusiastic of all has been Professor Hudson, the gynaecologist. He first came as a Cambridge undergraduate, and after morning flight he'd nip straight back on the train to train the university boat crew! When he was in Australia for eight years he had on his bedroom ceiling a blown-up photograph of a skein of geese, which he'd taken when he was out with me just before he left.'

With the improvements in transport, shooters now tend to visit Frank for shorter periods—'generally three days at the most. But many are so keen they come very long distances just for one flight. And with such a variety of people I've been down the marsh on all sorts of vehicle, including a pushbike, motorbike and sidecar, London taxi, minibus, Land Rover and Rolls Royce. The Roller had the plate JCB1 because it belonged to the boss of JCB diggers, who came with his son in 1959. He had the first hundred JCB registrations.'

But not all customers have been welcome, especially the model who nearly killed Frank. 'The previous week she'd been in the *Sun* paper in a bikini in the snow. Obviously that didn't provide enough excitement for her because she nearly shot me head off, and when she handed me the gun back at the car it still had two cartridges in it!'

Fortunately, Frank has never had any real troublemakers—not that they would have presented great problems because our guide is well used to awkward customers. When one of his three sons is on the bill as a professional wrestler Frank sometimes works as a bouncer on the door.

Neither has he suffered the indignity of a major fall or being seriously stuck in the mud. 'There was one very soft place where bombs had been dropped, but luckily I felt it in time and hurried on before I sank. It's the only thing you can do. But Pat Hovendon, a great big chap, dawdled and got stuck. He thought it was quicksand and was screamin' away so I had to rush back and pull him out.

'There was a time when I was lost, in snow and thick fog. I walked out round this semi-circular bank. Comin' back I thought I'd cut across and hit the bank on my right hand. I was looking out for this old Queen Mary trailer bridge across the creek but I missed it by the depth of the fog—only fifteen or twenty yards. Luckily I came across a sandy area I recognised and knew I had to follow the creek back. I wasn't too bothered by it, but I was 2½ hours late and Peg had a search party out. You should always let someone know where you are, and when you are due back.'

But even if you know your precise position, there is always the risk of injury on the marsh. Mud might be soft, but when there are so many gutters and creeks to jump or negotiate the occasional mishap is almost inevitable. Take the time in the late 1950s when Frank was with a party on Terrington Marsh. 'There was a drum in the middle of a dyke to help get across it. I held a stake this side of it so that people could take a short run and then grasp the stake to help take off, bounce onto the drum and jump straight off to the other side.

'Gordon Aveling, then aged eighteen, preferred to do it without the stake. He was wearing a loose-fitting oilskin, and as he took off he looked like Dracula. He half jumped and half slipped off the drum and then landed flat, short of the other side, with a colossal splash in a mixture of mud and water. We all fell about laughing until we realised that he had injured himself. Gordon took it very well, though unfortunately he had dislocated his shoulder; however, we were lucky to have Dr Watson from Whittlesea with us, and he looked after Gordon on the way to hospital. They had to ring Gordon's parents for permission to operate, as he was under twenty-one. Luckily, the only time I've hurt myself in waders was in December 1992, when I sprained me ankle.

'Another time when company was useful was when Tom Carter was bringing

After the flight—Frank (centre) and friends in the early 1970s

'When I went back he was shiverin' and almost blue with cold'

up the rear in the dark and for some unknown reason stepped out of line into a deep creek. When he was strugglin' around tryin' to get out a local joker came by and said: "Oi, you can't cross there, it's fourteen feet deep". Poor Tom lost his gun and his glasses, and when he drove off he didn't dare get out of second gear because he couldn't see. Fortunately, his things were recovered at low tide.'

But Frank's fowling has been the source of much good humour, too. 'When Bob Tall used to call to say he was on the way I'd be in dead trouble if I woke the family, so we devised a code and I slept downstairs next to the phone. When it rang Bob simply said "Quack, quack" and all I had to do was say "Quack, quack" back. If anyone had seen us they'd have thought we were mad.'

Once a group of fowlers left Frank to spend a few days with Bill Powell on the Solway. But before they went Frank slapped some mud on their waders and said: 'Tell Bill that's a present from the Wash'. Some weeks later Frank received a small .22 ammunition box from Bill Powell. Inside were some wigeon droppings along with the message: 'For Frank. Here's some Solway fall-out for you'.

Another veteran fowler who has provided considerable amusement is Arthur Nightingale. Peg remembers the day he first arrived. 'When I opened the door he was standing there in a leather flying helmet and said "Where can I park my

Messerschmitt?'' Well, I thought this must be some sort of big joke as I'd spent much of the war trying to shoot these things down! But it turned out Arthur had come in a *three-wheeler* Messerschmitt, one of those bubble cars. He's a wiry, but little man.'

Frank especially recalls one time he took Arthur out shooting. 'It was on a foggy, bitterly cold mid-December day in 1958, when the marshes were frozen hard. I put Arthur on an island and later heard him take a shot. When I went back there he was, shiverin', blue with cold and about to dress. All his clothes were neatly piled on the ground. It turned out he'd shot a pinkfooted goose and dived in to get it because he did not have a dog with him and the tide was taking the bird out.

'While he was still naked a goose went over. He picked up his trusty BSA but his thumb was too cold for him to get the safety catch off. He dressed then, and said he was quite all right. He did stagger a bit as his feet had got numbed by the frozen mud, but after walking about forty yards his circulation came back. As soon as we got him back to the pub Peg ordered him into a hot bath and afterwards gave him a drink of hot milk, rum and sugar.

'The most remarkable thing was that when I met Arthur in the gun room next morning he said, in all seriousness, "I'm taking a towel with me this time, Frank". Perhaps he thought it was normal practice to dive in after your kill.

'Another time Arthur even offered to retrieve a friend's two ducks, and we were laughin' like anythin' as he looked so funny, being short, starkers and up to his knees in sea asters. He swam to the first duck but could not find it, then he swam to the second, which was much farther away, and found it immediately. The fowler who had shot them was so pleased that he gave Arthur the duck.

'Arthur's a very good sport and does everythin' by precision. He even cuts up his breakfast like a surgeon, where most fowlers would gobble it up. I wonder how he got on when he stayed at The Bull, Long Sutton, where you would have as many as fourteen rashers of bacon on your plate! A bit different from "Donny the Dustbin" Evison, who even ate the rinds left by other breakfasters. One day friend Fred refused his pudding there, and after the landlady had left the room Donny shook him by the throat and said: "Don't you ever refuse anything!" '

But leaving aside the humour and hospitality, Frank has also managed to provide many Guns with great sporting memories, not least their first goose. 'Most people really come for the geese. Duck such as mallard, teal, wigeon and pintail might be the mainstay nowadays, but they are far easier to get. The pinkfeet and greylags take much more outwitting.

'The trouble is the geese have moved a lot in recent years, especially since most local farmers started growing cereals rather than spuds and sugar beet, and with all the mild weather there's been far fewer birds around. There's no doubt we'd be a bit slim if we 'ad to rely on eatin' what I've shot these last few years. It's ridiculous that we still can't shoot the brent geese even though they've become so common.

'But most people don't mind the lean bags. Anyway, some of 'em are more twitchers than shooters and are quite happy just to watch everything around them. The lack of serious wildfowlers is more worrying. We have 350 members in the Fenland WA, but there's not the youngsters comin' into the sport now. I don't think they've got the patience we had and now there's so many other easier things for them to do.'

One of the shocks for the newcomer is discovering that fowling is best in foul weather. When it's clear and calm wildfowl tend to flight high and out of range, but when it's raining and blowing a gale birds come driving in low and give the Gun more of a sporting chance. Even better is a blast from the east, for then Britain often fills with fowl in retreat from icy mainland Europe. When this happens Frank's east-coast patch is often first landfall, and—while of late he admits to puffing a bit—you can bet your waders that he will be the first to sniff the birds' arrival. He insists that he will 'be out there as long as I have breath'. And with his love of fishing to accommodate too, his home at Tydd Gote will never be much more than a roost.

FROM THE ARCHIVES

Vulnerable Norfolk

BUT the sea by its beating, washing, overflowing, and tearing, is sometimes so outrageous as not to be kept in by its banks.

From William Camden's *Britannia* (1586, revised 1789)

Fishermen-fowlers

IN the days of Colonel Hawker, very few gentlemen sportsmen knew anything of wildfowl shooting, and fewer still cared for it. Those who did, however, were perfect enthusiasts, but, generally speaking, the sport of sea-shooting was unknown almost completely to the vast majority of shooting sportsmen. The few selected spirits who indulged in it for the mere sport of the thing kept the fun amongst themselves, and virtually the vast bulk of wildfowl and seafowl which were supplied to the markets were shot by professionals. These men were sea-fishermen, who, when hard weather turned up in the back season, took to their big guns as regularly as clock-work, and, as there were but few of them, all told, the fowl were not much harassed, were therefore pretty tame, and the consequences were to the birds disastrous, for the men, though badly armed and badly equipped, scored heavily upon their serried ranks.

Lewis Clement ('Wildfowler'), 1884

FROM THE ARCHIVES

Recovered From The Sea

MARSHLAND is a peninsula almost surrounded by navigable rivers and an arm of the sea; the whole in the widest part but ten miles over. It contains 3,000 acres, and has over its many cuts and canals not less than 11 bridges. It contains seven villages, all whose cattle it feeds beside the sheep. These are Emneth, Terrington, Tilney, Walpole, Walsoken, Walton and Wiggenhall, which intercommon on Tilney Smeeth. The level surface of this tract and other circumstances seem to argue its having been recovered from the sea. Spelman tells us that there were within his memory two general overflowings, one of the salt, the other of fresh water. By the latter, as appeared before the commissioners, the inhabitants sustained damage to the amount of £42,000, the water not breaking down but overflowing the bank to the height of at least a foot. The present mode of banking by a substantial brick wall fenced with earth, hath been found most effectual to resist the tides, whereas the value of the estates was almost yearly laid out in the old way of embanking. Great improvements have been made on the coast by embanking; Captain Bentinck recovered 800 acres of saltmarsh, now arable.

From William Camden's *Britannia* (1586, revised 1789)

Sutton Bridge lighthouse

MUCH-TRAVELLED LUMINARY

JOHN BURRAGE

LIGHTHOUSE KEEPER OF THE CHANNEL ISLANDS, ENGLAND AND WALES

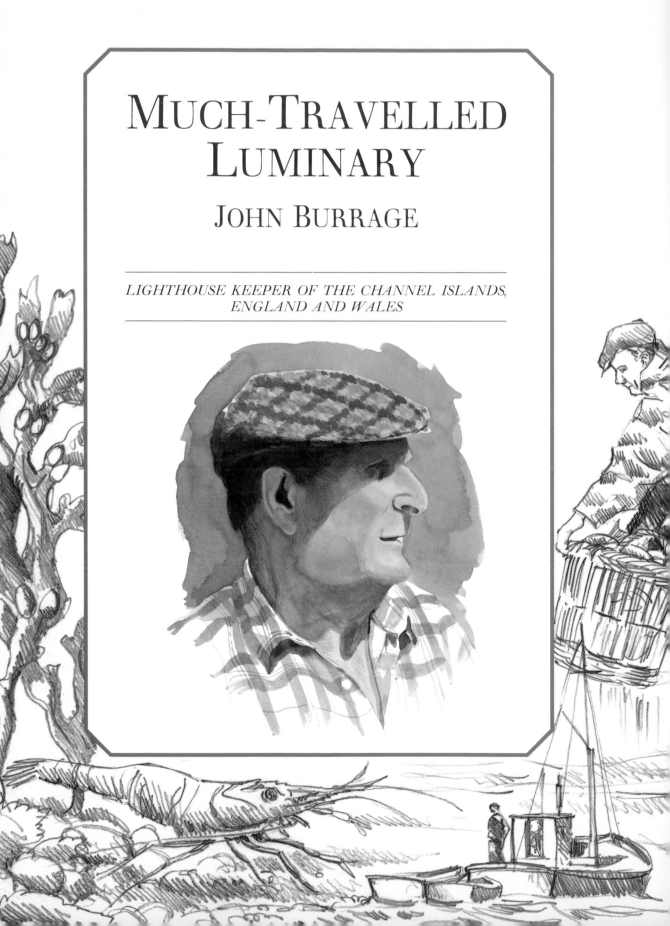

The Smalls Lighthouse

FORGET the pipe-smoking old beardie, nodding in time with his fishing float or peacefully filling his diary while the decades drift past his one untroubled window. Think more of twenty-four-hour, year-round commitment, life even more unsettled than Britain's notorious weather, and willingness to be stationed anywhere at any time. This is what lightkeeping used to be like, and no one knows better than John Burrage, who had no fewer than thirteen postings during his first eleven months as an SAK—supernumerary assistant keeper.

But then, as a child John Lewis Burrage knew nothing but lighthouses, for when he was born on Alderney, on 15 February 1923, his father was keeper of the Casquets light. And there was always salt in the Burrage veins, for Grandad was a fisherman.

John was one of only two children, but whether this was because lightkeeping paid poorly or because there wasn't much room in the keepers' quarters, I am not quite sure. Anyway, John and his sister left Alderney in 1928 when their father was posted to Nash Point, near Marcross, South Glamorgan. They lived in a headland cottage next to the light.

When he left school at fourteen, John was back in the Channel Islands, where his father had again been posted. There he did two years apprenticeship as a motor mechanic for Gallyon & Sons, before returning to Nash with father. Fortunately, in Wales he was able to continue with his indentures, at Llandow Airport, 'servicing Spitfires, Hurricanes and so on, for five bob a week. When I went there Mum bought me a pair of dungarees costing 4/11d.

'I wasn't called up because I was in a reserved occupation, but all my mates were and I felt left out, so I got fed up and kept on at the foreman for release. Eventually I was allowed to go, and joined the Royal Armament Corps, then the 15/19th King's Royal Hussars tank regiment.'

During the war John saw a great deal of action in Europe and Palestine. He was not injured, but had a very lucky escape when the early Challenger tank he was driving was hit by an 88mm high-explosive shell which blew the barrel off and badly damaged the rest of the vehicle. 'It was very upsetting in the tanks with headphones on because all the time you could hear them saying things like "Old Johnny's got it". All your mates were being killed around you.'

John spent much of the war in Norfolk and Northumberland. 'The winter of 1942–3 was particularly cold and I remember goin' out choppin' firewood with the sergeant at Rothbury. Put me in the hospital that did. I was holding a log which the sergeant hit with the axe, but he also split my leg. I was in Newcastle General Hospital, where the rats were runnin' around under the bed. But it was only temporary Nissen hut accommodation and we had good treatment. Army patients who were allowed out had a special uniform with sky-blue jacket, white shirt and red tie, so that people knew you were a soldier in hospital and would be nice to you.

'I was in Egypt when demob came in December, 1946. That was a horrible place, with Jews against Arabs. The roads were too bad to take tanks so they gave us armoured cars. As you came out with your demob suit all done up in a parcel, spivs offered to buy it. Some of the lads tricked them by filling their packages with dirty underwear before selling.'

John returned to live with his parents, now at Withernsea lighthouse, near Hull. 'I had three months leave, but in January Father said I ought to make my mind up about what I wanted to do. So I applied to Trinity House.

'I went to Blackwall, London for training. We had to learn everything, doing a fortnight at a time on things like soldering, carpentry and cookhouse. You had to get tickets in all sorts—radio beacons, engineering maintenance, and so on. And all the time you were liable to be called away.

'My first posting was to Coquet, near Amble in Northumberland, on 13 February 1947, during that bitter winter. There were three of us and we were so cold we used to put a house brick in the oven, wrap it in cloth and take it to bed. As supernumerary assistant keeper I went round relieving people who were sick or on holidays. My wages were very poor and we had to buy our own food, so I was always starvin' and used to write home to mother to bake me a cake.

'During that first year my stations included the Nab Tower (Solent), Needles (Isle of Wight), Flatholm and Lundy (Bristol Channel), South Stack and The Skerries (off Anglesey), St Anthony (near Falmouth) and Eddystone (in the

John was in Egypt before demob in 1946

On the steep steps of Lowestoft lighthouse, where John is now part-time keeper

Channel, south of Plymouth). You'd come ashore after, say, two months and have a telegram waitin' for you with instructions where to go next. There was no proper record kept of where you went as a super, and you couldn't leave all your stuff at one place until you were made assistant keeper, which I was when on the Needles in 1948. At the time I was so fed up with all the moving I was going to jack it in. A keeper's always had to go where they send him, else he's out on his ear. A transfer could come any time—even with the Christmas cards. And your children would have to change school.'

After two years on the Needles, John had over three years on the Bishop Rock (Isles of Scilly), before moving on to Nash Point (his father's old station) for ten years. In 1963 he was made up to principal keeper and assigned to The Smalls (off Pembrokeshire), but before he could get there he was transferred to South Bishop. Four years later it was off to the Skerries, and in 1971 he was posted to Hartland Point (North Devon), 'but that was another place I didn't get to because I was sent to Cromer (Norfolk). In 1975 I went to the Lizard (Cornwall) and retired from full-time work in 1983. But then I was lucky to get this part-time job, as attendant at Lowestoft. It's fully automated here so I just work sixteen hours a week cleanin' up, polishin' brass and keepin' an eye on everything. I hope to stay here as long as I can. They've been very fair with me here.

'It's very sad to see all the jobs go with automation. When I started, lightkeepin' was lightkeepin'! You really had to do everythin'. Now it's all gone to pot and the staff's not so dedicated. In my day the men would never let anybody down. If you went into a shop, ordered a hundred pound's worth of goods and said "Can I pay for it next week?" they'd almost always say OK. But now you'd get the thumbs down.'

There have been many changes in lightkeeping during John's time, not least in transport. 'I was on the Skerries when they started using helicopters to lift you in and out. I never liked it, but at least it meant that you weren't stuck on a light when the weather closed in. And it was often safer. My father was principal keeper on the Eddystone light when the supply boat landing oil and coal was so low in the water she was swamped and capsized. He grabbed one of the men by the hair, but had to let go else he'd have gone in, too. Eight men drowned. None of them were wearing lifejackets. Only the coxswain was saved, but he died in hospital.'

Living conditions, too, have changed greatly. 'At Nash the only water we had was from the roof and every drop had to be pumped up from an underground store, so it was never fresh. There wasn't a lot of it, either. Once a fire gutted the engine room and the fire brigade took all our water to fight it. They had to come back later and refill the tank. Also they did more damage than the fire, smashing everything to get in, the windows to let the fumes out, and our big compressors to avoid an explosion. The fire was caused by an engine fault.

'At Nash there was no electricity or flush toilets, only Elsan buckets which you had to empty over the cliff when the wind was in the right direction! Once my four-year-old son swallowed a ha'penny and I had to tip up all the buckets lookin' for it.

'Lighting was all by hurricane lamp and we had to use the crude white paraffin—light mineral oil—in the house: same as in the engines. How my wife, who came from London, put up with the smell I'll never know. Also each keeper was allowed six ton of coal a year for the Rayburn. When they sent round each spring to ask how much was left it was always "Nil", else they'd dock any over from your allowance.

'Food was a bit of a problem before fridges. But I used to get a dozen jamjars, buy 10lb of stewin' steak, cut it in chunks, put it in the jars, half-fill them with water and cook slowly in the

'At Nash we emptied Elsan buckets over the cliff'

At Bishop Rock it was 'a real eye-opener to watch those great big rollers coming in'

oven for two or three hours. I'd end up with eight jars topped up. When they were cool I melted beef dripping and sealed the tops. Delicious!

'On the rocks I always used to insist that all three of us sat down to a midday meal together, and we took it in turn to cook. Breakfast was your business. Today nobody bothers much.'

With a fairly restricted diet, lightkeepers have always welcomed occasional food parcels from caring communities. John particularly remembers those sent by local schoolchildren at Christmas when he was on the Bishop Rock. 'We used to get things like half a bar of chocolate, an opened packet of tea, and so on: anythin' they could find to fill it up. But we always wrote back and thanked them.

'One day on the Skerries three of us were havin' dinner when there was a knock-knock on the door. "Who on earth is that?" we said. When I opened up, there were two young girls there with a box. One said: "My father's compliments and please may we have a picnic on the island?" They'd come out in their boat and there were three chickens in the box.

'On the South Bishop we got six cockerels to fatten for Christmas. They used to drive us mad crowin' at four in the morning so we had to put them in a box too small for 'em to stretch their necks. But they became so attached to us, followin' us around everywhere, we couldn't kill them and gave them to a local farmer.

Pause for thought: John awaits the helicopter to take him to the Skerries for two months

Old lighthouse bulbs are ideal containers for John's model ships

'At Nash, Dick Packer decided to keep pigs so he went out and bought a sow. One day this bloke brought a boar down to service, but Dick used to suffer with a bad back and so on this day his wife Molly asked me to help. Shortly there was a litter of thirteen or fourteen. Then one mornin' I got up and heard all this squealin'. Dick had all his furniture out in the yard, bar the table. He was only castratin' the piglets in his kitchen!'

Fish have always provided a welcome supplement to the lighthouse keeper's diet, and John was among those who used to catch them with a kite. 'The frame was made from bamboo or rocket sticks, and beneath the float we had lures made from strips of chamois leather soaked in red ink. I worked the kite from the light gallery and the line was the length of the tower, so that when the kite was in my hand the fish laid comfortably on the set-off down below. Then I'd bang the gallery rail with a spanner so that the cook would come to the window below me, halfway up the tower. He grabbed the fish when I pulled it up and swung it into him. At the same time he'd check the line and throw it back out. We could only catch small fish like this, though kites were once used for other purposes too, such as taking in mail on the Bishop Rock. I've even seen papers and strawberries and cream come in this way. But you had to be careful on the Needles because there was rocks all round, so you had to wait for the wind to be in just the right direction. We had some lovely bass there.'

John's dangling skills also proved useful for another purpose. 'I had this old 28in bike which I decided to take down to the Bishop to strip down and clean up. But the very next day a ship came to offload oil and coal and I had to get the bike out the way pretty quick. So I put it on the winch and swung it out on the

Father used to catch lobsters in brass rabbit snares

wall. After that everyone going by used to say: "Look at that bike up there!" Goodness knows what they thought.'

Fortunately, John has never injured himself badly on a light, 'but I've seen quite a few visitors fall down the steps and hurt themselves. At Nash, Father once had Bet Davies crack her head as she went out the door. She was the guest of Hurst, the magazine and newspaper man, who used to have a lot of stars over.

'The only death I heard of on shore was when the son of Jack Beal, a lighthouse keeper father knew, was killed trying to get birds' eggs from the cliff.'

Occasionally the lightkeeper may need to help people in distress nearby, such as the time at Nash when John was on duty at night. 'I went out into the yard and it was pitch-black. I was just lookin' up at the light, which is the first thing any keeper would do, when I heard this faint cry—"Help, help!" Turned out it was a little boy on the cliff. Strictly speaking I shouldn't have left watch, but I asked my neighbour to look out, and with my brother-in-law Tommy Mather, who was on holiday at the time, hurried off to help.

'We went about a hundred feet down the cliff on a rope and said to this lad: "What's up, mate?" He said his friend had tried to climb up and had fallen thirty feet. He was in a hell of a state, so Tommy stayed with him while I went back up to phone the doctor and get warm drinks and blankets. Turned out the lad had broken ribs and a punctured lung. And it was a good job we got them both out quickly as there was a flood tide and they would almost certainly have drowned. Afterwards I had very nice letters from the boys' families, and the coastguards sent me ten bob, five shillings of which I sent to Tommy.'

But gratitude is not always readily forthcoming, such as the time when John was showing some visitors around Nash. 'I saw these people along the beach and the tide was flooding. I knew they were already cut off, so I grabbed a rope from the pig-sty and rushed down to lead them to safety. But when I got there they said: "Mind your own bloody business." I never did know what happened to 'em, and at the time I didn't care.'

Wildlife, too, sometimes needs a helping hand from the lightkeeper. 'On the Casquets, Father had perches on top of the lighthouse for exhausted birds to rest on. And on the Skerries the RSPB got us to light up the tower and we were paid for it. But even with the lamps goin' you could pick up a couple of bucketfuls of birds of a morning. They were mostly small ones, but some were bigger, such as shearwaters. They'd crash into the wall or even the main light, which attracted them. It was worst during migration, when lots of birds were on the move.

'At the Casquets Father used to catch lobsters in brass rabbit snares. He found their holes at low water and dangled a piece of fish in front of them.

'Father also made rag mats from old hessian coal sacks. One spring morning he was outside at this and after a while went in to brew the tea. When he came back out he was just in time to see a bird making off with a piece of his material. Later on he found the nest and it was made entirely of cloth, by a rock pippin [pipit].

'We had puffins nesting in the rabbit holes on the Skerries, and at low water we could get over to the island they were on. Once my mate promised a little girl a puffin's egg, but when he put his hand in the burrow he got bitten.'

Birds can also pose problems inside a lighthouse. 'At the Lizard, small ones such as sparrows used to get in the engine room and you just couldn't get 'em out—they only want to go up all the time. A bird in the light was bad news because the mantles which we once used were so fragile: even a moth would break one. This was with the incandescent oil burners, like a Tilly lamp, in the days before electricity. Each mantle only lasted about four days, anyway.'

Fortunately, four-footed pests rarely get inside a lighthouse, but John recalls one very surprising encounter at the Needles. 'One day in 1947 my mate said "Somethin's been chewin' at my bacon". But we couldn't find anything so we set a trap. Still nothing. Then the potatoes were gnawed so we put poison down. Then there was no more damage, but we still didn't know what had been eating the supplies.

'A while later my mate said "I think I'll bake some bread". So he went down to get one of the 7lb bags of white flour which we used to buy from the depot.

'Once us keepers towed an old bungalow bath across the fields'

John Burrage used over 8,000 matchsticks to make this model
of the Bishop Rock Lighthouse

And there inside it was this big black rat—dead! Apparently, just before I got to the Needles a cattle ship had been wrecked there and the rat had come from that. It had swum across onto our landing and lived on grease and stuff for four or five months. Eventually it must have got onto the tower and up the steps.' Obviously the lighthouse cat had not done its stuff, which was a bit 'off' when 'the firm' even used to pay for pussy to go on the train when a man was transferred.

Once in a while the lighthouse keeper will encounter sea mammals, too. Sadly some are dead, such as the porpoise which John found at Nash. 'The Cardigan museum came down and measured it up. Then they asked me to dispose of it by burning. It was a smelly job, but it went well with all the fat, and they gave me ten bob for my trouble.'

Other visitors come by appointment, to see how a lighthouse functions, for Man has long been curious about this apparently peaceful occupation. In particular, it makes a good day out for schoolchildren—though some can be distinctly tiresome, such as the party of sixty, five- to seven-year-olds which John tried to entertain at the Lizard. 'They were packed into the tower like sardines and I started to give them the usual patter. But about halfway through I could see they weren't taking any notice, so I suggested to the teacher that I cut it short. But she insisted I carry on as they were taping it for discussion back at school.

'At the end I asked the children if they had any questions, but the only one was: "How does Father Christmas get in?" All they were puzzled by was the lack of a chimney!

'Anyone new to lightkeeping can easily be frightened by the power of a stormy sea. At Bishop Rock, when a big sea struck the base of the tower it used to shudder and your tea would spill into the saucer. Then the mercury would spill out the bath for the lens and we had to go round, sweep it up, put it through a mutton cloth and back in the trough.

'One Sunday afternoon I was 180ft up cleanin' the brass on the Bishop when it suddenly went dark and a huge sea came right over us. We had ten days there trying to get off. But that's nothing. I knew a chap had three weeks stuck on the Wolf after the end of his watch. And the time you was over came out of your leave!

'I've not seen any damage to a light, but in my days on Bishop Rock you were not allowed to paint the walls inside so that you could spot any cracks which might appear. It's a real eye-opener there if you watch those great big rollers comin' in. But you get used to it. Sometimes your bunk would shake, but you'd generally drop off to sleep again.

'But it could be pretty near impossible to sleep in fog. We had Tonite charges goin' off every three minutes. When you were on duty there was a little bell went to remind you to press the plunger. Some stations had five-minute intervals between. We had boxes and boxes of charges and detonators—the IRA would have loved 'em. But each man only took up enough for his watch. And on the Bishop Rock you had to jump out of bed and go out in wet oilskins to get your share from store.

'At the Coquet it was more sounding for snow rather than fog. But once or twice it was bitterly cold at Nash, too. Once us three keepers towed an old bungalow bath across the snowy fields to get enough supplies to last a while.'

Not surprisingly, each lighthouse has a lightning conductor, which runs right down through the tower, with branches off. John recalls its effectiveness at Bishop Rock. 'Bill Pickering was sweepin' down the iron stairs for his morning routine when lightnin' shot down the conductor, past him and out the kitchen stove with a tremendous crack. But Bill was unhurt.'

Like many lighthouse keepers, John has made mats and models during quieter moments. Some of his ships are in bottles, but one is in a bulb which lit the South Bishop in the 1960s. Perhaps most impressive is his model of the Bishop Rock lighthouse, painstakingly made from eight thousand matchsticks. It even has a flashing light with the right 'character'—two flashes every fifteen seconds, which distinguishes it from all other lights.

Despite all the hardships, John has been very happy working for Trinity House. His favourite light was Nash. 'After all, I did over twenty-five years there altogether, and I got to know everybody in the village of Marcross, and some in Llantwit-Major, five miles away.' Now he is very content at Lowestoft, despite the handicap of having only one lung, which makes climbing the steep stairs very exhausting. He readily admits: 'I could never live away from the sea. I like to be able to open a door or window and see it any time I want. And whenever I have a bit of puff I walk down just to be next to it.'

FROM THE ARCHIVES

Mere Place Of Passage

HOLYHEAD is a wretched place to a stranger in winter time. In summer weather, I daresay, walks over the hills, and rows out to sea or in the harbour, may offer some inducements to visitors to while away their leisure pleasantly; but in winter the hills are bleak, rugged, and bare; the wind blows as though it meant to spend all its strength over that particular spot; and walks and rows are, moreover, out of the question. There are several inns, and one or two hotels, but no society; in fact, Holyhead is but a mere place of passage for people who are bound for Ireland. All these things considered, we were very glad we had the yacht to roost in. After all, there are few places more cosy than a yacht's cabin at night when the evening meal is over, and the chatty smoke is entered upon.

From 'Wildfowler's' *Shooting, Yachting, and Sea-Fishing Trips* (1877)

ON COURSE FOR SURVIVAL

JOHN PATIENCE

FISHERMAN AND FERRY SKIPPER OF ROSS-SHIRE

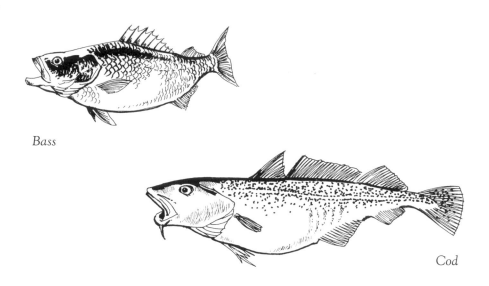

Bass

Cod

THERE was never any doubt about the course John Patience would steer. Not only had his family fished out of Avoch since the mid-eighteenth century—as far back as records go—but also 'times were so poor you *had* to go to sea'.

Not even great tragedy halted the Patience tradition. In 1850 John's great-grandfather and his three brothers were in their fishing boat, a 20ft open yawl, when it capsized off Rockfield, Easter Ross. 'All were drowned, except the youngest, who clung to the upturned boat all night. Their father went to bed and never rose again: he died of a broken heart. They were all buried here in Avoch. You can see the stone now.'

Such stories have survived easily in this insular community where one lady, who was in her nineties when she died recently, knew no less than seven generations of the Patience family.

Avoch's current population of some 1,500 is much the same as it was just before World War II. John recalls: 'A lot of the boys married away from home after the war, but we had plenty of incomers to compensate'. However, newcomers have always struggled to be accepted, as John's wife Rebecca (Betty) knows only too well. 'I'm still regarded as a "driven fish" because I came here from Greenock in 1950.'

The couple now live but a stone's throw from where John was born, on 23 May 1921. One of six children, John attended Avoch Public School. 'There were about thirty in my class and as many as three hundred in the school, with a lot of families workin' on the farms. I liked school and did well, but most of us couldn't afford to go on for highers. It was very hard then. Sometimes you went barefoot for six months to save your boots for the winter. I remember the master wanted us to dig the school garden in April even though eighteen out of twenty of us had no shoes.

'Every Saturday we used to go for wood for the fire. We'd walk about a mile up to the big wood and bring back sticks in hessian sacks on our backs. Very little coal was used then—maybe a bag a month. Boats from Sunderland brought it in and took back seed potatoes. Up here we used to get two crops of tatties in one year, lifting the first in mid-June. It's very fertile ground.

'I think this is called the Black Isle because of the colour of the earth. But it could be because the snow never lies. Incidentally, an old painter told me that the name "Avoch" is an abbreviation of the ancient name which had twenty-six letters. We have a very distinctive dialect here and a lot of the words come from the Gaelic. Many, such as "bojack" for squint, are the same in Polish. Others are close to the Norwegian, such as "ma" for seagull and "greeten" for crying. Avoch was always considered a very safe port and people came from all over Europe to deal here. Once we had a linen mill which attracted much trade with Holland. And in the nineteenth century there were still five bootmakers and seven wheelwrights here.

'Electricity came in the 1930s, but ninety per cent of people had the paraffin up to the war. There was always a lamplighter about the streets. My uncle was one, but Grandfather didn't think much of his efforts. He used to say: "There's never been a meen [moon] since me son started the job!" You see, a good lamplighter wouldn't light up if there was a good moon, to save the council's money.

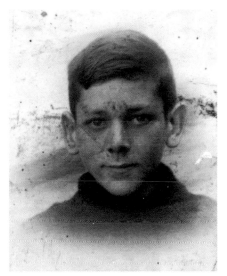

'But although we were poor we did have some fun in my schooldays. Once I had first prize for the most imaginative essay, but when teacher read it out to the class everyone laughed because I'd put the tallies [real names] in for local people.

'Another time we were doin' a concert and five of us ten little nigger boys were named John Patience—all related to Great-grandfather. We got together and decided to poke our tongues out to the audience, all at the same time. Everyone was doubled up with laughter, and the Head was behind us so he didn't know what was going on. But later on he found out, and gave us six of the strap each.

Even as a schoolboy, John was always thinking of the sea and fishing

'Although it was tough then you always got your food and was healthy. No tinned stuff then. It was all porridge, fish and tatties. Once a week our main meal was rice pudding with currants in, and another day it was salt herring and tatties in two separate pans. The west coast people always put the tatties on top of the fish in one pan.'

'We also used to poach for game, using snares, catapults and ferrets, to supplement the food larder. Once we got a hare, and when we gutted it the dog who followed us gobbled the whole insides: it was revolting. I tried to sell the hare to the banker's wife, but she said you don't gut hares when makin' soup. Alas, no pocket money for me.'

Luckily John's headteacher was good at navigation and taught the boys a lot about the sea. 'We were already very involved in fishing and used to catch the big bolger herring from the beach, but sometimes we went in little skiffs after the main kessock herring. The bolger net was six foot deep and anchored to seaweed on stones so that the weed would break first if we got snagged up. Bolger were taken mainly in August on the big Lammas tides, and on the March wrapper when they spawned. Us children mostly only caught a couple of pailfuls.

'On a bigger boat each man had six nets apiece, and maybe a spare net too, so there would be thirty-six or more all tied together, with a float between each and stretching for a mile. We used to drift any time from August to March, following the fish, from Beauly down to Inverness and round to Invergordon. The birds would show us where to shoot our nets. We used to have a fine wire, like a piano string, with a 5lb lead on the end, and put it over the stern to test the fish. It was just like cutting cheese where the herring were so thick.'

'Every Saturday we used to go for wood for the fire'

When John left school at age fourteen, he had to dig potatoes on local farms, at 9d a hundredweight bag, for the few months before the fishing started on 1 May. 'I started on the 45ft *Lily*, number INS 121, which had a thirty-horsepower Kelvin paraffin engine. We went after herring on the west coast, around Uist, Harris, Barra and so on, and were away eight weeks before you got a weekend. When you came back home the first thing you noticed was the height of the grass. It was very barren on the islands where we fished, but there were lots of yellow irises in the peat bogs.

'I was on the *Lily* from age fifteen to eighteen. The first time I was at sea I was supposed to get thirty bob a week as cook—young boys always started like this—but I took a thirteenth share instead. There were six shares for the boat, which had all the gear and so on, and six for the crew. The cook was supposed to get slightly less, but when we were squaring up, with the skipper's wife doin' the counting on the table, one man suggested I had the same as the rest since I was a big lad and did as much work as some of the men aboard.

'We ate well, with stews and roasts. They always looked after the grub for the people at sea. We had a pudding just about every day and I think I gained two stone in the first year. Going to the summer fishing the boat took a big ham, a big round of cheese and some salt fish. Them who smoked got two hundred cigarettes each, and pipe smokers got black twist.

'We usually put in to anchorage to get some peace, because if you put on the shore you'd generally get people pokin' about the boat. If we went on a long trip, like to Mallaig to discharge herring, we used to hoist a big foresail while keeping the engine running. Then we could keep up with the drifters, at ten knots or so—without the sail we only managed six or seven knots.

'In winter we used to go out in shallow water on lochs all along the west coast, where we'd use ring nets, which were three hundred yards long with a purse in the middle. And up to 1939 we used to roll horsehair on the knee to make long lines. Some which we ran out from the boat had as many as a thousand hooks on and were baited with lugworm. They were weighted at one end with a flag marker, and laid on the bottom, mostly for flatfish. At Inverness in 1895, when Dad was just thirteen, they filled the boat with flounders fishing like this. And even as late as the 1960s, David Jack—the last of the line-haulers here—is said to have drowned because he had so many herring and so much gear aboard. But now the fish are nearly all gone. The trawl's killed it off.'

Sharks, too, fetched a good price. John's boat used to get £12–14 for a porbeagle. 'They were sent to Italy for eating, along with threshers. But one thing we didn't like was sailfish because their oil would rot your nets. Once at Castlebay we had seven through our gear, so we had to wash and dry the nets quickly. Also old whales used to come up by us as close as you are now—and the smell of them!'

Understandably, when fish were so plentiful they were very much cheaper. 'Some were taken to market at Inverness, but others sold locally. A cran [3½cwt] in quarter baskets would make from about seven shillings, according to quality and demand. Sometimes there was so much choice the buyers used to help themselves and virtually make their own prices. The Swedes used to come over and give us only two bob a barrel for the mackerel. Cadgers hawked herrings and flounders about the streets, sometimes bartering for eggs. Granny did it till she was seventy-seven, though this was mostly before my time.

There were lots of irises in the peat bogs

Eighteen-year-old John Patience,
Royal Navy Reservist

'Father and me also gathered a lot of whelks and sent them down to Billingsgate. Towards the end we got as much as £20 a hundredweight for them, but when I was a lad it was only 3/6d. We'd boil them for three or four minutes and eat them cold. There was also a good oyster bed here up to the 1890s, but all the boats came up from Rochester and Gillingham and trawled it out. Now all you see is empty shells.'

Unfortunately, the fishing life was mostly unexciting for young John and his friends. 'At Castlebay, on Barra, your best entertainment was singing hymns and gettin' a cup of tea in the Church of Scotland hall on a Saturday night. There was no baker there, and the bread was green by the time it came in from Glasgow, so toast was very popular! And in January and February, when we used to go down to the south firth [Firth of Forth] for the herring that spawned there, the highlight for the four of us fifteen- to sixteen-year-olds was being taken home to tea after the church service.'

John was still on the *Lily* when war broke out in 1939, but since January that year he had been training hard in the Navy Reserves, having pretended that he was eighteen to get in. After six weeks training with the Royal Navy, at HMS *Victory* in Portsmouth, he and Hugh Patience were the only Avochies called up for the King's Review at Weymouth in July. 'But when the war started, two hundred others were called up from here.

'I joined the destroyer *Vanessa*, and after just five days on patrol got right into the action. There was a tremendous flash ahead when an Estonian boat carrying vats of tallow from Godenia was torpedoed. We fired depth charges and managed to bag our first submarine. And we sank another two when taking thirty thousand fresh troops from Greenock to relieve the garrison at Gibraltar.'

In 1940, despite a German sabotaging some of the ship's guns while in dry dock, both *Vanessa* and John were ready for action at St Valery en Caux, as escort to boats carrying soldiers escaping from France. He was in the first convoy going south around Dover after Dunkirk and, as a quartermaster, watched in horror as every ship except his was sunk by fifty German Stukas (Junker 87s). 'Our skipper had good presence of mind and was zigzaggin' to escape, but the *Vanessa* was badly damaged. We were opened up like a tin can and the engines were out of line, but no one was injured. Funnily enough, "stukas" is also an Avochie word meaning standing like a statue.

'After major repairs we were hit again, on 14 July 1941, off Yarmouth. One bomb went down the foremost funnel and another took the side out, with the loss of fifteen men, mostly Chiefs and POs. Most of them were buried at Caister. As we were towed in, the banks of the river were crowded with men applauding us, all the way up to the yard.'

While on the *Vanessa*, John played left-half for the ship's football team and they lost only one game; thus he put in valuable practice for when he would become a professional after the war. Team captain was Neil Paterson, who played for Dundee United when he was nineteen.

In July 1943 John again narrowly escaped death, on the cruiser *Cleopatra* when it was torpedoed by an Italian submarine and twenty-five of the six hundred crew were killed. 'I was the torpedoman and had been on duty all night when, at 6.10am, this chap felt sorry for me and said he'd listen out while I washed up. After we were hit, at 6.25am, I found him dead without a mark. I was very lucky.'

By 1944 John had been made up to chief petty officer and was on the block ship *Alyn Bank* for the D-Day landings. 'We sunk her with depth charges, and the two wreckers and myself were taken onto a landing craft. As I clambered aboard I heard a lad shout out and I said: "You're from Inverness". He asked me where I

In 1946 John embarked on a brief professional footballing career

was from and gave me a new pair of boots. I often wondered what happened to him.'

After demob in 1946 John went back to fishing. He also played football for Inverness Thistle and Ross County, of which he was captain, before becoming a professional centre-half for Arbroath, then in the second division, for 1947–8. 'We each earned four pounds a week plus one pound for a win and ten bob for a draw. At the same time I was getting five to six pounds a week working as a civilian, second lorry driver, in the Arbroath naval establishment.

'I only came home because my oldest brother wanted me to help with the family's new fishing boat, the *Forager*. In 1950 I earned just £12 for an entire sixteen-week trip.

'Later we had the *Primula*, and when that was sold I had two years on someone else's boat. Fishing could still be very good in the late 1960s. I specially remember one night-time I was on board the *Integrity* with skipper George Jack when we came across a big shoal of herring in Loch Callan, Uist, Outer Hebrides. I was in the wheelhouse watching the echo-sounder. When I spotted the fish I shouted "For'ard", for the man to put his searchlight on, and the top fish were so frightened they rose ten to fifteen feet, out of the water. We put out the ring-net and the boat *Rosehaugh* picked up our end.

'The net was too heavy to lift, so we towed it to the shore, in water three to five fathoms deep, over sand. We filled eight boats with fish, but there weren't any more to take the rest as most of the fleet was away fishing elsewhere. So we had to tow the rest of the herring back out and release them, by then dead with the crush. Altogether there must have been 1,500 cran [one cran equals 37½ gallons], about 250 tons, in the net. Apart from the *Integrity*, *Rosehaugh*, *Mondhlaigh* and *Zephyr* from Avoch, the boats filled were *Falcon* and *Flourish* from Hopeman, and *Fortitude* and *Catherine* from Kyle and Kyleakin. Boats often used to give each other spare fish in the old days.

'From 1972 to 1984 I was skipper of the ferry on the 1¼-mile crossing from Cromarty to the Highlands Fabricators' oil construction yard at Nigg, Easter Ross. This was when all the rigs was gettin' built and you always had to be on your toes. It was very exactin' work, and at one time I never missed a sailing in

HMS Vanessa, *on which John Patience nearly died*

'*Whales used to come up by us as close as you*'

On board Primula *John welcomed the New Year, during the biggest season of kessock herring*

fifteen months.' This was a remarkable feat of seamanship because, at the height of some storms, John's ferryboat was believed to be the only one in service in Scotland.

But John would never take a risk. He could remain at sea because he knew his patch intimately, which was just as well for a man who routinely made the double crossing three times a day, and as often as ten times in twenty-four hours during the early days of the Nigg development, with over five hundred highly paid workers in his care. 'Good knowledge of tides made all the difference, especially the big equinoctials in spring and autumn. My main worry was landing at both piers with the strong currents and no shelter.'

The only serious accident which happened while John skippered the ferry was when a man broke his leg. 'Like everyone, he was told not to jump ashore until the boat was tied up properly, but he did, and got his leg trapped between the boat and the pier.

'I can't remember any bad accidents on the fishing boats. Luckily, I never went overboard, but I've had to haul a couple of men in. There's been a couple of lucky escapes, too. Once my brother's oilskin had to be cut off him to stop him goin' round the winch. And uncle had a big cod hook in his boot when the line was shooting over the side. Luckily the boot came off and went overboard instead of him. Running a line of a hundred cod hooks was a very dangerous job!

'Sometimes it was bitterly cold too, workin' with bare hands. At first we wore kerseys—heavy wool trousers—but for Saturday nights we had a bonnet [cap], serge trousers and lovely jumpers, hand-knitted with four long needles using fine wool and always decorated with anchors, diamonds and ropes. The women had a special leather belt for the knitting.

'I think we had heavier frosts before the war, but it was healthier then. No wonder there's all the colds now with the intermittent weather. The bitter winter of 1962–3 wasn't so bad in the Western Isles where it's sheltered. We had mostly nice calm weather and were even sunbathin' at Stornoway.

'But 1946–7 was terrible. The burn was all iced over, and down here on the beach a lot of wading birds were frozen to the ground. I've always studied the birds and they've certainly helped me with the fishing. The old women used to say: "When you see the seagulls with black bums there's no fish in the sea", because then they'd hang around the chimneys after the crusts.

'I think there's more variety of birds around here now. The finches are really coming back and we've even got the reintroduced red kites around. But the funny thing is there's only ever been about thirty turnstones here all my life, never any more.

'When we went down to Whitby and Scarborough we used to get about twenty-five to thirty exhausted birds of all kinds come aboard. They were mostly wee ones, but some as large as a pigeon. We tried giving them whisky and water, but they all died. Nowadays in many areas it's much easier for them on passage because they have the oil rigs to rest on.

'We also used to chase the solan goose [gannet], which showed us where to cast our nets. Sometimes they sat on the water stuffed with herrings, which they'd spew up at our approach because they were so heavy and couldn't fly.'

Today John no longer chases across the sea, though he still nets the occasional fish for home consumption. 'The flavour of a wild salmon or trout is different

'When you see the seagulls with black bums there's no fish in the sea'

altogether. And mackerel is all right fresh, but a herring in season is the tastiest of the lot.

'Some old people still regard the salmon as bad luck—"cold iron", the opposite to "touch wood". There's always been plenty of superstitions here. If you forgot something when you went off fishing your mother wouldn't see you turn back. Swan Vestas matches were also regarded as ill omens. And if you met anyone who you thought was going to bring you bad luck, you had to turn round three times.'

Much of the fishing folklore is contained within songs which John has made up and occasionally sings to his three children and grandchildren. 'I've had the tunes in my head since I was a child.' Hopefully much of the luck and lore has been passed down to John's only son—also John, who, in having a skipper's ticket, maintains strong family ties with the sea. With such a rich heritage in his cabin, it should be many years yet before Avoch runs out of Patience!

FROM THE ARCHIVES

Hordes Of Herring

THE largest shoals of herrings appear in the North Sea, and on the east coast of Scotland, where sometimes great moving masses of fish are seen, that are quite two miles broad, stretching for three or four miles along the coast.

From F. & L. Duncan's *Life In The Deep Sea* (1898)

ONE OF THE LUCKY ONES

FRED MORRIS

*NAVY SIGNALMAN AND COASTGUARD OF
PORTSMOUTH, GREENWICH, THE ISLE OF MAN,
LINCOLNSHIRE, SUSSEX AND SUFFOLK*

AFTER a tough upbringing and several narrow wartime escapes in the Royal Navy, Fred Morris joined the Coastguard in search of the quiet life. 'The idea was to put me feet up and suck away on the ol' pipe while looking out. Also I didn't want to work with men who weren't Navy. I needed people I could yarn to.' And so it turned out, for Fred was always one of the lucky ones.

One of nine children, Fred was born on 23 March 1913, at Portsmouth, that ancient centre for seafarers. At the time his father was a dockyard worker, but also a Royal Fleet Reserve stoker who was called up in 1914 and stayed on as a regular until 1933.

Fred's earliest memories are of 'a Zeppelin passing over Portsmouth in the Great War, and the Armistice Day celebrations at Guildhall Square, with lots of tanks and guns.'

At twelve years old he went away to the Royal Hospital School, Greenwich— 'No 5 company, No 109. I had to fight the first day I was there because somebody else wanted to be cock of the walk. There was no heating in the dormitory and the discipline was severe, but we were always hungry and often tempted to help ourselves to extra rations. Once I had twelve cuts of the cane for "a daring raid on the galley through the skylight adjoining the dormitory". I was the leader of a gang called The Four Aces.

'At Greenwich we used to have our own names for lots of things, especially food. Margarine was "flop", meat "fat wang" and bread "toke". Each loaf was cut into threes and the bottom crust, the "cur", was always the most desirable.'

However, Fred did have the opportunity to earn a little pocket money, as tenor horn in the band. 'We used to play for garden parties and got about half-a-crown each.'

At the age of fifteen, Fred went to the Royal Navy's training school, St Vincent at Gosport, Hampshire, as 'boy, second class'. 'At Greenwich I'd been bottom of the bottom class, but now I was in the top ten selected for the advanced class. After a month I was transferred to *Ganges*, at Shotley, for signal training. When I left Shotley at sixteen and a half years old, in 1930, I received about 1/6d a week, after everythin' such as uniform was deducted.

'I joined the *Emperor of India* as signal boy at Spithead in January 1930. It was blowin' a gale as we sailed for Portland, Dorset, and it was the first time I'd been on a ship as well as the first time seasick. We went to Spain and came back to Pompey in April.

'Then it was back into barracks to await draft to the battleship HMS *Queen Elizabeth*. We saw the old battle cruiser *Tiger* leaving Gibraltar flying her paying-off pennant. At Malta we split up and I joined the *Revenge*, later transferring to *Resolution* and then back to *Revenge*. I came home as signalman on the *Coventry* in 1932.'

In 1938 Fred married; and he was on the *Boreas* when it was nearly sunk by three Spanish government aircraft. 'It was a very near miss intended for Franco's

(Opposite) *Sixteen-year-old signal boy Fred* (standing) *and his friend Harry Dale at HMS* Ganges

(Below) *On the lookout: Fred, station officer at Lowestoft*

'We found the fin of a big bomb sticking out the sand'

flagship. AB Long was in one of our boats returning from Canarias after delivering survivors from a cruiser sunk. Then I remember seeing him laid out dead in our wardroom, with a hole in his chest as big as your fist. With everyone standin' around, the scene was just like the death of Nelson in that painting on my wall. And two other men were injured.'

When war with Germany was declared, Fred was in the court martial room of RNB Portsmouth, taking the exam for yeoman of signals. 'It was just after 11am on Sunday and the bosun of signals came in to give us the news.

'For the first three years I was on convoy duty on the east coast and in the Channel. I survived three sinkings in the North Sea and never got my feet wet! The *Port Denison* and the *Esmund* were bombed, and the tanker *Ahamo* was mined at night. I'd only been on the *Ahamo* six hours and was asleep on my own in the lounge. The top of the stairway was blocked by a big bookcase which had fallen down, but I had my torch with me and managed to spot a hole just big enough to scramble through.

'I left convoys in 1942 and joined the escort carrier *Activity* training pilots on the Clyde. Then it was Russian convoy duties before going off to Cochin, China, and Sydney, Australia. I was chief yeoman from 1945 and transferred to the Fleet Air Arm in 1949—the worst thing I ever did.'

Fred joined the Coastguard in 1956, on the same day he left the Navy, at the age of forty-three. For five years he was one of a team of four at Ramsey, on the Isle of Man. 'To me it was just like being on signal station, and my pay was £4 19s 6d a week.

'It was very quiet at Ramsey. In five years we had only one casualty. It was always windy there, but at least we did get to see the TT races for nothing.'

Promoted to station officer, Fred went to head a team of three at Mablethorpe, Lincolnshire, where it was just as quiet. 'From 1961 to 1964 I lived in the old district officer's house, and all around the walls was the tide-mark of the 1953 flood—a line of salt about four feet from the ground.

'One day we found a beached whale, which we were supposed to bury, but it was a bit big for us so we got the local corporation to do it. Apart from that, the only excitement we had at Mablethorpe was when we found the fin of a big bomb sticking out of the sand on the beach. We thought it had been accidentally dropped and called in the bomb people, but it turned out that it had been on display outside the local RAF air cadet corps place and someone had moved it for a prank.

'Our lookout at Mablethorpe was on top of a sandbank and one day we had to abandon it after subsidence. It was only a nightwatch station anyway, but then it was reduced to "occasional lookout" status, which meant keeping watch if the wind was force four or above, or if the weather was foggy or otherwise bad. So I moved to Lowestoft, Suffolk, as station officer, to a "continuous watch" station where we had a team of five.'

Although Lowestoft was much busier, even there Fred found plenty of time for his hobby of making model ships in bottles, some of which he still has. 'See this one: I dropped it and the sail fell off, so I filled it with water and called it the *Mary Rose*.'

Among Fred's other mementoes are a couple of the old bronze Coastguard wreck service tokens, which used to be given to bystanders for helping out in an emergency and could be exchanged for cash at Coastguard stations. 'We used to keep them in store at each station, but they were all withdrawn in the seventies when an advert appeared in *The Lady* magazine—a collector offered £40 each for them because they'd become so collectable. Some were issued by the Board of Trade, others by the Irish Free State.'

At Lowestoft Fred brought off a few rescues by breeches-buoy, such as in 1970 when the first man off the beached trawler *Grenada* 'got a ducking because he weighed fifteen stone and our line dropped a bit'; but there were no major incidents. Fred's only experience of tragedy was the death of a fisherman, as described in the chapter on Tommy Knott. 'He'd been trapped by his leg in a groyne and was drowned by the incoming tide despite the combined efforts of all the rescue services. Anyway, it was about three weeks later before the storms had abated sufficiently for me to go down and get my line back. I happened to be there when divers recovered the man's leg—from the knee down only and still in his boot! The power of the waves must have snapped the poor devil free.'

But that really was the exception. For most of the time Fred managed to find the quiet life which he had expected, and much more energy was expended in

Sounding off: Fred with an old fog horn from his collection of coastguard equipment

chatting to the public than dealing with disaster. But even holidaymakers occasionally brought surprises. 'One chap came up to me with an empty bottle and asked if he could have some sea water. He only thought he had to pay for it! A simple soul—up from the country I suppose, and probably never seen the coast before.

'It was just as quiet at Selsey Bill, Sussex, where I was station officer 1973–8.'

Since retirement in 1978 Fred has lived at Horstead, Norfolk, where he is surrounded by artefacts and memorabilia and has indulged his great interest in Navy and Coastguard history. Not only has he compiled a book on the British admiral, but also helped many folk trace service records. There is no doubt that he has had many a lucky break, and now he is trying to give something back to the way of life which served him well. In this he has been much more fortunate than his coastguard brother, who died at the age of sixty-five, only three months after retiring as station officer at Wick.

FROM THE ARCHIVES

Expanding Portsmouth

As the great town enlarges its borders it draws nearer and nearer to our parish of Portchester. In another 50 years it will probably have reached us. And then much of the interest of the old place will be gone. The walls of Roman masonry will doubtless be left standing, and the Norman keep will tower for perhaps another century or two above the mud flats and the flowing tide. But the glory of the parish will have departed. The wild-fowl will no more visit the harbour-shore. In very hard winters when the ponds and lakes are ice-bound they will again seek, as their ancestors have done for centuries, the open salt water of the harbour, but they will only look and pass on. Choice wild-flowers will be searched for in vain; the so-called improvements of town life will drain the last patch of marshland where once the teal and widgeon congregated in countless numbers, and the beautiful beard-grass will be gone. The samphire will go with it, and the adder's tongue, and the Deptford pink will no longer open its beautiful crimson petals on the rough stretch of marshy waste which borders the vicar's glebe beside the ancient mill.

From John Vaughan's *The Wild-Flowers Of Selborne And Other Papers* (1906)

ACKNOWLEDGEMENTS

Most of all I would like to thank the sixteen main characters in this book for giving so generously of their precious time and divulging so much personal information. Secondly, I must thank their wives and families for providing excellent hospitality, as well as occasionally helping to nudge the flagging memory. Then I wish to express my gratitude to all those people and organisations who set me on a course to track down my subjects, especially Warren Davis, Gary Davies and Harriet Dean of the National Trust; Chris Harbard of the Royal Society for the Protection of Birds; Mrs J. Wilson of Trinity House; Paul Ridgway, editor of *Flash*; Robin Sharp of the Royal National Lifeboat Institute; Mike Floyd, editor of *The Lifeboat* magazine; J. J. Smith, Cromer RNLI; Michael Chapman, Lowestoft RNLI; Capt Philip Toghill, Ramsgate RNLI; HM Coastguard London; Ian Fraser, editor of *Coastguard* magazine; Paul Lane, Principal Inspector HMCG; Tony Laws of the British Association for Shooting and Conservation; Robin and Erica Rolfe; Gus Britton, Royal Navy Submarine Museum, Gosport; Mrs R. Hough, the Pandora Inn, Mylor Bridge, Cornwall; Tim O'Nions, editor of *Shooting Times* and *Country Magazine*; Alastair Murray, Ray Collier, Colin Foote, Brian Dunn, Ron Bennett, Trevor Charlton, Mike Coultas, John Marchington, John Darling, Jerry Williams, Les Arnold, Arthur Nightingale and John Fair. Finally I wish to thank Sue Hall, my editor at David & Charles; Philip Murphy, for his evocative illustrations; and my wife Carol for her help and companionship on distant voyages.

INDEX